D1169432

PRAISE FOR *TOOLS FOR TH.*
PARENT OF A CHRONICALLY-ILL CHILD

"Must read for any parent coping with their child's serious illness. Provides critical insights for maintaining continued hope and resilience. A true story about a remarkable woman. I recommend it to all my patients struggling with chronic illness."

Susan Taterka, MSW, LICSW, ACSW

"*Tools for the Exceptional Parent of a Chronically-Ill Child* is the record of a journey in the life of a child and her family, and of the dedication and love that it took to care for her. The book is also a guide for parents of children living with serious illness not only addressing medical challenges, but also offering pathways for the protection of the 'person' who is suffering. Living with an ill child is a huge burden, and often not adequately shared by partners, family or friends. This book covers it all with frank, powerful clarity. It is both an affirmation of life and a sobering discussion of the hurdles that chronic illness creates. It provides a testament to the efforts required to help a sick child grow into adulthood with uncertainty about the future. I was deeply affected by this book, and you will be as well."

Richard J. Grand, MD, Boston Children's Hospital

"A wonderful guide for one of the most difficult roads in life's journey. Shirley Riga's courage and openness in the face of these challenges is contagious, and her hard won advice will help other parents cope with similar difficulties. The emphasis on taking care of one's self in the midst of it all is a timeless and important lesson for all caregivers."

Karen Osborn, author, parent of a chronically-ill child

"It is truly healing for others who know the roller-coaster of emotions and have travelled even a short parallel path. Many obstacles along the author's difficult path force her to find help and make tools to forge ahead. She stumbles and falls. Reading along, I stumble onto nuggets about acceptance and forgiveness. For the first time since my sister's illness and death, I can breathe deeply. This incredible journey, told from the heart, offers strength and comfort. Riga has taken her own great pain and transformed it into comfort for others. What a beautiful gift!"

Carol Luck, author of *Heroines of the Kitchen Table: Stories of Survivors*

"I just finished the book and I haven't been able to stop crying. So many mixed emotions. I'm angry, sad, heartbroken and happy all at the same time. You're the real fighter in this story."

Anonymous parent

Tools for the Exceptional Parent of a Chronically-Ill Child

Shirley Riga

STRONG VOICES PUBLISHING

Strong Voices Publishing
P.O. Box 731
Medfield, MA 02052
www.strongvoicespublishing.com

Credits:
Cover design by Terry Houseworth
Mother Mountain poem by Shirley Riga

This book is based, in part, upon actual events and persons. However, some characters and incidents portrayed and the names used herein are fictitious. Dialogue and events have been recreated from memory. Any similarity of those fictitious characters or incidents to the name, attributes or actual background of any actual person, living or dead, or to any actual event is entirely coincidental and unintentional.

Author disclaimer: All experiences in this book are my own and do not represent a professional's advice or suggestions. My only expertise is as a parent of a chronically-ill child. The author does not dispense medical advice or prescribe the use of any technique for physical, emotional or medical problems without the advice of a physician, either directly or indirectly. The intent of the author is only to offer information of a general nature to help you in your quest for emotional and spiritual well-being. In the event you use any of the information in this book for yourself, which is your constitutional right, the author and the publisher assume no responsibility for your actions.

ISBN: 978-0-9905361-2-3
eISBN: 978-0-9905361-3-0
Library of Congress Control Number: 2016934180

Acknowledgments

My writing has been cathartic on many levels for many years. I have always contended my daughter has been my teacher, and my classroom has been parenting my two daughters. But, honestly, my classroom began years before and parenting was my graduate course. Therefore, I want to acknowledge first my then husband and the two wonderful daughters we created together. As I grew and turned to trusted friends, I leaned on them and they withstood my weighted life challenges.

A deep and appreciative thank you to our pediatrician, physicians, therapists, social workers, physical therapists, occupational therapists, nurses, specialists, music therapists, speech therapists, hospital staff in general, ambulance drivers, practitioners, phlebotomists, ministers, visiting nurses, mentors—the list is endless of those in the helping profession who have given us the gifts of kindness and caring. To my four-legged friends who have given me comfort and joy. To my beta readers for their love and time and feedback; to Thea, my ghostwriter, editor, confidante, and soul mate for all her support and love; to my daughter and her husband who have blessed me with two wonderful, delightful grandchildren, and to my teacher.

Table of Contents

Mother Mountain

My strength I carry in my tall
thick walls of stone.
I weather the hottest heat and chilliest cold.

I stand as witness to the lives of people,
animals, energies that pass by me,
over me and on me.

I reach high to heaven and am made
up of the very essence of Mother Earth.

I am majestically beautiful and
starkly abundant in my stature.

I carry within me memories of days
long past and futures to come,
yet represent the presence of what is.

MY STORY

Monday, December 14, 1981

There's something strange about the lights of Boston as we lurch past them. I glance at Mark but he's concentrating on finding the hospital. Lisa lays in my arms, oblivious to the thin pale pulsation of the lights and the pounding in my heart.

It's easy to think over the last seven weeks. Lisa's birth had been normal. Since she was a second child, I knew what to expect. At three weeks she had caught a bad cold which almost became pneumonia. She had her first X-ray and was put on antibiotics. Though her cold improved, I worried about her—she seemed to cry a lot. I made another appointment with the nurse practitioner. She checked my baby over and assured me she was fine, that her ruddy complexion would go away. When Lisa slept, I was grateful for the peace.

I had trouble breast-feeding and felt so inadequate about it. I inquired about therapy to deal with my self-judgment but was put on a waiting list.

At her seven-week checkup, Dr. Kapher questioned me about her complexion and ruddy color. He did blood work. "Probably no problem. I just want to be sure."

After the blood was taken, he asked me to wait for the results.

The kids in the waiting room were curious about this new baby. With their wide eyes and innocent curiosity, they looked at her color. "Is she wrapped up in yellow like a doll present?" They reminded me of her sister Michelle's excitement over the fast-approaching

Christmas holiday. I was glad I already had my shopping done.

Dr. Kapher is a tall man, over six feet. Usually, he has a happy face. He came out of his office and I followed him back to the examining room. I looked around. The nurses looked concerned.

Dr. Kapher wasn't smiling. "A problem showed up in the blood work."

"What do you mean?" I held Lisa a bit tighter.

"I'm not altogether sure but her liver function tests are elevated. This needs to be addressed by the specialists," he said. "That's what they're there for." I could see wrinkles in his large face I'd never noticed before.

He had already called Boston Children's Hospital. "They're expecting you immediately, like this afternoon. How soon can you get there?"

"I don't understand," I began. I felt myself receding into a faraway space. "Boston's almost two hours from here."

"You must leave at once." He pushed the phone towards me. I stared at it blankly. "You can use our phone to call your husband and make arrangements."

His words echoed in my head as I dumbly repeated them into the receiver. Mark said, "I'll give my mom a call, let her know what's happening and we can drop Michelle on our way out of town."

Boston Children's is a teaching hospital which means eager residents and interns are everywhere. We walk into the Emergency Room and go through triage. A phone call is made. A team of doctors show up. They take us into an exam room and begin interrogating us about every minute detail of my pregnancy, Lisa's birth, and the previous weeks' events. We go through the lengthy process of getting her admitted.

Lisa is settled into a large crib with high metal railings. During the next 24 hours, Mark and I answer the ongoing flow of doctors' questions. Lisa undergoes blood work, a CAT scan, an ultrasound. I must have repeated her birth story a dozen times.

We're directed to a room at the Gardner House next door to the hospital. It's a tall apartment-style building whose purpose is to house the parents of the hospitalized children. Each room holds two twin beds, a bureau, and a chair. The nightstand is illuminated by a large panel of overhead fluorescent lights. There's a shared bath down the hall and kitchen next door. I stop briefly in front of the mirror over the bureau and notice the haggard hollowed look on my face.

I feel like I'm in the Twilight Zone.

Tuesday, December 15, 1981

Mark and I are at Lisa's crib by 6:00 a.m. I pick her up and rock her in my arms, grateful to be with my baby again.

The doctors enter as a pack with an intense dark-haired man in the lead. "I'm Samuel Gold, Chief of Pediatric Gastroenterology. Did you two sleep?"

We shake our heads.

"I know this is very sudden. You did the right thing coming in right away. We don't know what's happening yet. We'll have to do some tests to be certain."

Mark asks our burning question. "Is it that serious?"

Dr. Gold stares at him. "Yes, this is life-threatening. And we have to be sure of our plan of action."

They leave. Tests are scheduled throughout the day.

Wednesday, December 16, 1981

More tests. Doctors check Lisa over, studying her color, taking her vitals. No one knows anything yet.

I want to yell at them, "Do something!" But I'm silent. We just have to wait.

I hold Lisa in my arms and cry.

Sunday, December 20, 1981

We've been staying at the Gardner House for five days without knowing anything other than our baby's life is slipping away.

Dr. Gold enters, again followed by his pack of doctors. "Here's what we believe is happening with Lisa. Of course, we can't be sure until we surgically go in and confirm our suspicions."

It's the first time I hear the word surgery. I remember thinking they can't be serious, she's so tiny. Some antibiotic will fix it. I look at the faces of the doctors. There must be at least seven of them.

"Her liver is not draining the bile it should be draining which causes a blockage in her body. What we surgically need to do is go in directly at her liver. If we're right and there's no drainage, we need to create drainage. Otherwise, she will not survive. Dr. Univeri is an experienced pediatric surgeon who has done this procedure before. We have scheduled the surgery for 7:00 a.m. tomorrow morning. Now what questions can we answer for you?"

They are serious. They want to operate on this tiny little baby of mine. How could they? His words are flooding through my brain like a tsunami—liver problems, surgery. She's just a baby, one who was born with all her beautiful parts—10 toes, 10 fingers, two large brown eyes. After a birth, relatives and friends are supposed to surround you with oohs and aahs, showering the newborn with diapers and nighties and undershirts, all sized impossibly small like doll clothes. Everyone knows what the experience is supposed to be.

It isn't supposed to be this—talk of surgery and worried-looking doctors.

Monday, December 21, 1981

The hospital lobby has a bustle to it but I can't hear anything. I start focusing on the hum of the elevator motor. It has a certain rhythm—something predictable in a world spinning out of control.

When the surgical nurse arrives and takes Lisa from my arms, my heart is still attached to her. This baby I bore had seemed the picture of health. Her ruddy complexion gave her a rosy-cheeked appearance. Giving her to the surgical nurse feels like pure abandonment. My heart is screaming but my voice is silent.

We head back down to the lobby to wait. And wait. There are magazines piled up on a corner table. I try to read. What is so important about which star is on another diet or getting a divorce? My eyes blur. The elevator hums. People whirl around me like cars on a highway.

At noon, Mark leans over. "Let's grab some lunch while we can."

"What if they show up while we're in the cafeteria?" I fret. "We have to stay here."

"I'll go get us something then." He stands up. "I'll be quick. Besides, Dr. Gold said she'd be in recovery for several hours after surgery. It's only supposed to be four hours."

"I'm not moving," I say. "I'll page you if they come."

Another 15 minutes pass with no word. Mark reappears holding a tray of sandwiches and slices of pie. We set up our little camp lunch and eat quietly as we stare at the elevator.

Another 45 minutes. Then, we see the surgeon approaching us. Dr. Univeri is older with thinning gray hair. He scans the room and spots us. I jump up.

"Everything went as expected," he says. "She'll be in recovery for three hours, but she's stable and that's important."

I'm feeling as though my heart will jump out of my chest. I hold on to Mark to stand steady. I'm feeling the first bit of relief I've had in days. The Twilight Zone will be coming to an end.

The doctor continues. "Now we watch and wait. So if you want to finish your lunch, go right ahead."

We have so many questions, but I don't know what to ask. Mark does. "What was done?"

"The gall bladder and biliary tree were dead—what we call necrotic tissue. It was removed and we connected her transverse colon, her intestine to her liver. This allows bile to drain from the liver as it would normally. The actual procedure is named the Kasai procedure after Dr. Kasai who invented it over 10 years ago. The next 24 to 48 hours will give us a lot of information."

"What do we watch for?" Mark asks.

"We follow her blood work, watch her color and all her vital signs." There is an audible pause. "I've done approximately 50 of these Kasai procedures. The success rate is 50 percent at this point. Hopefully with a good strong fight in her and her body's ability to heal, she will survive. She may be looking at a transplant down the line, but for now, she's stabilized."

I must have a blank look on my face. Transplant? He didn't really say that, he said that was a maybe. He said she's stabilized. That's a good thing, a great thing. The end of the tunnel is near. I ignore his 50 percent comment.

He continues. "I've already spoken with Dr. Gold and relayed the same information. You can go see Lisa in recovery on the fifth floor. They're expecting you." He shakes Mark's hand. When he just stands there, I realize he's waiting to shake my hand. We shake and then he turns and leaves.

Mark and I find the elevator and wait with several others. Once on the elevator, a slight, middle-aged Eastern Indian woman starts a conversation with us.

"All the tubes and lights and beeping machines are a little intimidating," she says, "but you will be able to hold your daughter. It's important to always treat her as a normal child, to discipline her as a normal child."

I'm exhausted from the sleepless nights and tension. "Are you talking to us?"

"I'm the pediatric social worker here to accompany you up to see your daughter. I'm here to support you in this process and if you feel the need to talk during your stay, I'm available."

All I hear is the elevator motor. Why is she saying all this stuff? Lisa is going to be fine now. That's what the surgery was for.

She continues. "Raising a child with liver disease should be like raising any other child. Does Lisa have any brothers or sisters?"

Mark answers, "She has a two-year-old sister named Michelle."

I chime in, not really understanding what this social worker is saying. "She's with her grandmother right now."

The elevator doors open on the fifth floor. Surgical Recovery. We're directed to wash our hands and put on surgical gowns. Lisa is lying flat on her back in an incubator, arms laid out like a cross, palms up. There are tubes and lines attached to both of her tiny arms. Her little chest is rising and falling with each breath looking like a bird's heart beating. When I see the surgical wrapping around her little belly, I'm shocked and almost start screaming. Oh my God, her little body!

The social worker starts explaining. "You're both welcome to take a seat and use the openings in the incubator to hold her hand and let her know you're here. Talk to her."

I'm afraid to touch her little body. Her chest heaves up and down. This is insane.

"She should be waking up any moment now."

Mark sits down and pulls me next to him. "When will we be able to hold her?"

The social worker looks at the pediatric recovery nurse for the answer.

"Another couple of hours and you can hold her and spend time with her. We have rocking chairs up here. Once she's stabilized, she'll be moved to the East Wing where you can stay with her."

"So we can come back?" I ask.

"By all means. Dr. Gold wants to speak with you. This has been a trying time for you and when you come back, you can hold Lisa. She'll be more awake then as well." The nurse smiles at me. "We'll take good care of her."

The social worker escorts us to the conference room where Dr. Gold and his team are waiting.

"Please." Dr. Gold gestures to the chairs.

We sit down.

Dr. Gold turns towards Mark. "The surgery confirmed Lisa has Biliary Atresia which is a liver disease that happens *in utero*. We don't know whether it's a virus that attacks the fetus or there's some other cause. We've taken a liver biopsy which we will study. Biliary Atresia is a very rare pediatric liver disease. There's no cure. A liver transplant is often necessary by the age of two." I can feel the clinical excitement as he elaborates on the rareness of her disease.

Dr. Gold continues. "The Kasai procedure is a solution that has allowed these babies to live. Complications arise though, because the liver is connected to the intestines where bacteria live."

I look at him not understanding. The surgery fixed everything, didn't it?

He continues. "Her condition will have to be monitored on a monthly basis. We'll be talking more about this over the next week or two, but for the time being, she's recovering. It'll be good if you spend time with her, hold her."

Mark and I just stare at each other. Then we're back in the hallway. I'm in a fog. I'm starting to grasp the fact that this is not over. The Twilight Zone descends again as his words filter their way into my brain. Monthly monitoring. No cure. Transplant. I make my feet move, one in front of the other dully like a robot. I glance at Mark. His face is ashen and drawn. I can tell that he's working to control his tears.

We head over to our room at the Gardner House. Even though there are two twin beds, we fit ourselves on one of them, holding each other, feeling stunned and drained.

As soon as I take a breath to relax, I feel nausea and pressure on my throat. "I'm going to throw up."

Mark jumps out of bed and grabs the trash pail. Lunch is sitting in my stomach. I violently retch. I collapse back in bed. My head is pounding; my sinuses start stinging.

We fall into a fitful sleep.

Tuesday, December 22, 1981

We're back in the conference room. Dr. Gold says, "We'll want to test both of you within the next few days."

I stare at him, slowly comprehending the implication of what he's saying.

He continues. "The liver biopsy indicated Lisa has a second liver disease called Congenital Hepatic Fibrosis."

"What!" I feel the blood rushing to my head. I didn't believe this nightmare could get any worse, but it can.

"This makes Lisa's condition extremely rare," he says. "This disease is secondary to Biliary Atresia. It's a slow degenerating disease. And," he looks at Mark, "the chances of you having a second baby with Congenital Hepatic Fibrosis are one in four."

I look at Mark. He's as stunned as I am. Is this my fault? Is it his?

"Because this disease is so rare, it's important we understand as much as we can about its occurrence. Therefore, it's really important we perform a gene study on both of you with your consent."

We sign.

Lisa is admitted into a regular room on the seventh floor. She shares it with another baby. I attempt to breast-feed her but just lifting Lisa requires managing all her tubes, IV lines and drainage bags. I rock her in the chair, so grateful to be holding her. So afraid of doing something wrong.

Once Lisa is fed and back in her crib, I call Michelle. I sit in the phone booth bent over my knees, holding the receiver close listening to Michelle in her high little voice talk about her two-year-old world.

Michelle is crying. "The fan fell on my big toe and it hurt so much. Nanny tried to fix it."

"Here's a kiss through the phone. I'm sorry to hear you dropped it on your big toe. It must have hurt." I use my voice to caress her sadness.

"When are you coming home?"

My eyes are burning. "Daddy is coming tomorrow to pick you up at Nanny's. Mommy has to stay at the hospital because baby Lisa is very sick. When you get home, be sure to give Tawny a big hug and kiss for me."

I've always loved dogs. I get such comfort from our golden retriever. I know Michelle does too.

"Okay, Mommy. Nanny said I can help her feed the kitties tonight." Michelle's voice sounds squeaky. I miss her so much.

"Sounds like you're helping Nanny a lot by being there. Daddy wants to say goodnight to you and then you'll see him tomorrow. Sleep tight, Michelle. Mommy loves you very much." I wipe my tears away as I pass the phone to Mark.

Wednesday, December 23, 1981

It takes courage to handle a tiny sick baby. She seems so breakable with a five-inch incision across her entire belly. The nurses encourage me to hold her as much as possible. She has cried and cried during this week in the hospital. She seems to get comfort from being held, but that feeling of safety disappears when someone takes her away for another test. It breaks my heart to see her body startle during each medical procedure.

The hospital floors are decorated with snowmen, Christmas trees and Hanukkah candles. Garlands hang in a festive attempt to counteract the heaviness of a floor full of seriously ill children. Mark is traveling back and forth, trying to balance staying with Michelle, working at our store, and coming into Boston. We stay in phone contact. Of all times for this to be happening, it has to be the holiday season.

I continue to struggle with breast-feeding. I think my anxiety has dried up my milk. I'm disappointed in myself because breast-feeding is one of the most important things a mother can give her new baby, especially a sick baby. I want so desperately to help her, to give her more than life—to give her health.

To wake up from this impossible nightmare.

I feel so alone here in Boston. I talk to Mark and Michelle every day. I cry myself to sleep most nights at the Gardner House. Mark is going to pick me up and bring me home. Christmas is looming. It's our tradition to spend Christmas Eve at his mother's house opening presents and celebrating over a large meal. My goal is to keep the holiday as normal as possible.

Will our lives ever be normal again?

Thursday, December 24, 1981

Conversation is so awkward with Mark's family. Holiday seasons and happiness don't mix with the sadness of Lisa's life-threatened state.

I want to just shrink away into a corner and cry. Instead, I go through the motions of unwrapping presents and acting happy.

I feel like a candy shell, all nice and shiny but empty inside. I long to be with Lisa. I've left her alone in the hospital. Michelle is in full swing with Santa Claus and all I can think about is how lonely and scared Lisa must feel.

I remember sitting in Dr. Kapher's waiting room patting myself on the shoulder for having done all my shopping before Lisa was born. There was no way I could have handled this Christmas if I hadn't done that.

Wednesday, December 30, 1981

The doctors have decided to discharge Lisa. I'm so grateful! She looks sickly pale with a drain sticking out of her right side. Her IV is still attached but it'll be discontinued shortly.

Her discharge instructions are long and complicated with prescription medications and follow-up guidelines with her local pediatrician. But even with that, it feels like a small ray of hope. Meds, checkups. That sounds doable. And if at two years of age, she needs a transplant, we'll arrange for that. We can get on with our lives.

I gather her into my arms and bundle her little body into the car seat. Mark's driving. He gets onto Storrow Drive and then the Mass Pike. I'm remembering—was it only a few weeks ago, that frantic drive into Boston on Dr. Kapher's insistence? So much has happened since then. I don't feel like the same person. How naïve I was then, believing a quick trip to the hospital would fix everything up. I've been fighting to not become a stranger to myself. Have I succeeded? I can't say.

Lisa's color is pink. She has a healthy glow to her, soft and satisfied like any other comforted baby. She has a pacifier in her mouth which she loves to suck on.

The words "chronic illness" float around in the background of my mind. I don't know exactly what they mean and it probably won't be a quick fix like mending a broken bone. We'll settle into a family routine, whatever it will be. And we'll get beyond this.

Wednesday, January 27, 1982

Our first post-hospital doctor's visit. Dr. Kapher is upbeat but thorough, checking all of Lisa's vital signs. He has blood tests done.

"She's doing very well." He palpates her abdomen with a serious look on his face. "Good, her liver is not hard. The blood is flowing."

I smile as I carry Lisa out of his office and we go home. I promised myself to not get my hopes up, but how could I not? Maybe the Congenital Hepatic Fibrosis will just go away.

She's being stabilized, he has said. When Michelle was three months old, I was giving her a bottle, baby oatmeal, and some baby fruit. Lisa is taking supplements of vitamins and nutrients. And medications.

Wednesday, February 24, 1982

Another doctor's visit. I'm wondering if we need these monthly checkups. Lisa's doing fine.

"You're giving her all the supplements?"

I nod my head. "And all the drugs. Are they all necessary?"

"Poor nutrition pretransplant can cause post-transplant complications." Dr. Kapher looks at me. "She's going to need a transplant someday."

"I know, I know." I guess I've been pretending to myself that living in a routine will make all the bad things disappear.

More and more, I'm learning what chronic illness means. This is my reality, preparing my baby daughter for a transplant when she's two years old.

Saturday, February 27, 1982

Lisa is sitting on my lap watching Michelle. I put her on a blanket on the floor on her back. As she tries to see Michelle, she rolls over, excited to watch.

In my mind, I compare their development, fearful of any delays in four-month-old Lisa. Should I worry? She was only in the hospital for a few weeks and besides, I'm very precise in following the doctor's feeding instructions and medication regimen.

Monday, April 26, 1982

Lisa is six months old. She still loves her pacifier and when I can get it away from her, she babbles out all sorts of baby sounds. I get Michelle to help me with Lisa's incision care so that Michelle understands there can't be any rough behavior with baby Lisa.

"Mommy, why does Lisa have a long line on her tummy?"

"Do you remember when Lisa was born and we took her to Boston and you stayed with Nanny? The doctors fixed her and made her all better. That's why we have to clean her tummy now." How do you explain to a two-and-a-half-year-old the reality of doctors, surgery and life-threatening diseases?

"Her tummy is big."

Lisa laughs. "Ahh, goo."

"Lisa, can you say 'mama'?"

She rolls over onto her back and looks at us.

I smile. "See, Lisa knows her own name. Isn't that wonderful?" I sit her up.

She wobbles over like an oversized egg. Her little belly is so distended it's hard to find clothes that fit her. She reminds me of Humpty Dumpty. Her favorite outfits consist of overalls held up by the shoulder straps with the sides open to accommodate her large belly.

I gather her up in my arms.

Sunday, June 20, 1982

I'm feeding Lisa regular baby food now. "Lisa, can you say 'mama'?"

Her little mouth babbles as she reaches for the spoon. "Goo ahh maa ahh maa."

I'm sure of it, she said 'mama'. She's definitely working on language. I want to call Mark and tell him.

With each day, life seems more and more normal. I feel like balking at the monthly doctor's visits, but even those have become normal.

Wednesday, July 28, 1982

It's the day after Mark's birthday. In a week, we're going to the lake in New Hampshire. We've rented a cabin that sleeps six and this'll be our first getaway since Lisa's diagnosis. Our lives have regained some constancy, with Michelle in daycare and Lisa growing.

Lisa is in my arms resting on my hip. She's happiest being held like that. We're at the back door overlooking the deck and the backyard. Her little legs hang hotly at my side. She's had a fever for three days. I decide to check in with the doctor before the trip.

The receptionist answers my call. "Come in this morning at 11:15. Dr. Kapher can see her then."

Dr. Kapher puts his stethoscope down after listening to Lisa's heart and lungs.

"I'll order blood work of her liver function tests. She has no other signs of a cold or flu."

"It's no big deal, right?"

"We need to rule out any other complications. Nora will give you the necessary paperwork for a chest X-ray. Get that done and I'll call you when I get the blood results." Dr. Kapher moves towards the door. "It should be just a couple hours before we see the results of the blood work."

Three hours later, Dr. Kapher calls. "Her liver functions are elevated. I've already talked with Dr. Gold and he's expecting you at Boston Children's first thing tomorrow morning. He thinks she has a liver infection."

A liver infection. Is this normal for a child after a Kasai? Is this what all these checkups have been about? I'm a little confused but I make the necessary arrangements for Michelle to go to her grandmother's while we prepare ourselves for another trip to Boston.

We cancel our vacation.

Thursday, July 29, 1982

How odd to be back at Children's Hospital. I'm remembering the first time, was it only seven months ago?

The doctors examine her and confirm Dr. Kapher's suspicions. Lisa is diagnosed with a liver infection and is admitted for 10 days on IV antibiotics.

I'm back at the Gardner House staring at myself in the mirror. Meds and checkups are one thing, but her being hospitalized again is a whole other story.

Sunday, August 8, 1982

We are home from Boston Children's. She needed IV antibiotics and she got them. It had to be done in a hospital because she's so young. It doesn't mean anything else.

I'm determined to keep our lives on track. It was one setback. Her supplements are helping keep her healthy.

"Lisa, say 'mama.' " I sit her up on her blanket on the floor. She uses her hands to maintain her balance.

"Ahh ohh." She looks around and reaches for her soft bunny. She tips over. I help her right herself.

Sunday, August 15, 1982

Lisa awakes with another fever.

"Bring her right in," says the receptionist at the doctor's office. "I've spoken to Dr. Kapher and he'll see you when you get here."

We go through the steps of another chest X-ray and liver function test and then home to wait for the results. A couple of hours pass.

The phone rings. "Lisa's liver function tests are elevated again. I've already spoken with Dr. Gold and he wants you to bring Lisa in tomorrow morning."

Monday, August 16, 1982

   Michelle is with her grandmother. Mark and I take Lisa to Boston Children's Hospital. Again, Lisa is diagnosed with a liver infection. A decision is made to keep her on the antibiotics for 14 days.

Friday, August 20, 1982

   As a teaching hospital, Boston Children's is a place where interns and residents as well as medical students observe and are part of examinations and treatments. Several teams of doctors visit throughout the day. I answer their questions, often repeating the same story over and over.

Monday, August 30, 1982

   I'm exhausted. She's had two liver infections in a month, and she's spent 24 days in the hospital. I'm hating hospital food and the too colorful walls.
   Lisa is discharged.

Wednesday, September 1, 1982

   This morning I'm waiting in the doctor's office. I say hello to a woman I know. She asks me how my new baby is, assuming all is well. I'm thinking she can handle the news since I know her. I tell her the truth, that everything is not fine. How the baby at nine weeks old had major abdominal surgery and was diagnosed with two liver diseases. As I hear my words, my stomach lurches with the hospital memories.
   The woman raises her hand and stops me in mid-sentence. With a look of horror on her face, she says, "Sorry, I can't deal with your problems." She gets up and leaves the office.

I'm devastated. What just happened? It feels like no one understands what I'm going through.

Saturday, September 4, 1982

Lisa again has a fever. We repeat the same blood work, chest X-ray and extended hospitalization on IV antibiotics.

Mark drops me off at the Gardner House again. Each time, I've been assigned a different room. This time I'm back in the room we had that first visit. For some reason, it feels harder. I remember how I threw up that first time. I'm looking at the wastebasket Mark brought to me. I have to hold my stomach to not repeat it.

I'm exhausted. The doctors say words like chronic illness and then go home to their perfectly healthy families. What do they know, what does anyone know of the reality, day in, day out, the relentless state of never knowing what's going to happen? I didn't sign up for this when I got pregnant.

When's this insanity going to end? Or is it not?

Thursday, September 9, 1982

Lisa is discharged. At home, I feed her, making it a game.

As I dance around the kitchen, she follows me with her big eyes and says, "Eh."

She's almost a year old. I remember when Michelle was that age; she loved her white blanket with a satin ribbon around the edges. "Blankee," she would say whenever she was upset. It helped her feel better.

"Let's try crawling. Would you like that?" I pick her up and we go into the living room where I rest her on her knees and hands. "Here's your bunny." When I wave the toy in front of her, she bobbles her head excitedly but doesn't move. She tries to and when she can't, she starts to cry.

Sunday, September 12, 1982

Her fourth liver infection. We're back at Boston Children's Hospital. Infectious Disease has been called in because of Lisa's recurrent liver infections. A decision is made to use several wide-spectrum IV antibiotics for five days in Boston and then Lisa will be transported via ambulance to our local hospital for another 10 days of IV therapy. The doctors are confident this will clear up the recurrent infection. But they add that her veins are compromised by the IV therapy and blood work.

Sunday, September 26, 1982

Lisa is discharged.

Friday, October 1, 1982

Michelle is three years old today. We have a small party for her at the daycare. She loves it there, especially her teacher Laverne. I bring hats and noisemakers, but the noise is too much for me and I have to leave the room. I'm supposed to be there for my three-year-old, and all I want to do is run away. What kind of mother have I become?

Thursday, October 21, 1982

As we approach Lisa's first birthday, the recurrent liver infections have continued. A few times her fever has spiked to 105 degrees. Gentamycin is the main broad spectrum IV antibiotic used, although it is highly toxic and puts her at risk for hearing loss. Dr. Gold hopes the IV antibiotic therapy will stall the infections.

Tuesday, October 26, 1982

Lisa is one year old today. Happy birthday, Lisa. I love you very, very much.

I take her out of her crib and put her down on the floor. She can sit now pretty well. I help her to a standing position. She loves it, as she holds onto my hand.

"Here, Lisa, you can be in your walker and watch everything Michelle is doing."

Thursday, October 28, 1982

I try again to put Lisa on the floor to crawl, but she doesn't move. I'm not sure what to do. It's like her torso is frozen. Does she have pain around her abdomen? I put her in her walker and her little legs flex in excitement. She grunts, "Eh, eh."

Monday, November 29, 1982

She has developed a fever again. We follow protocol and contact Dr. Kapher who contacts Boston and gets the insurance in place for our forthcoming visit. I tell him about my concern about her lack of crawling.

"Let's deal with the fevers first."

"And her speech? It's not progressing."

"That too can wait," he says.

I have become numb to this routine. It has almost become ordinary, like putting a child in a nice dress to visit Nanny. Only we put her in her carrier and take her to the hospital.

Today, it's a routine lung X-ray to rule out pneumonia. I'm standing next to Dr. Kapher as he explains the radiology findings.

He sucks in his breath. "That's really odd. The radiologist must have positioned the X-ray machine a little wider than usual."

"What?" I ask.

"Look at this," he says. "It's a radioactive isotope marker."

I ask him what he's talking about.

"There's a foreign object in your daughter's abdomen."

Tuesday, November 30, 1982

I'm holding a very hot baby. Mark's driving. I don't care she's not in her car seat. I don't care if we get stopped. She's very uncomfortable. It's all I can do to comfort her.

Dr. Kapher had said it's a small piece of tubing, possibly a drain that had somehow been left in her abdomen. "Maybe this is the cause of all her fevers," he suggested. "I've spoken with Dr. Gold. The team will be waiting for you when you arrive."

It's like déjà vu. It's almost a year to the day we took this same trip to Boston. Last time we were in a frantic state. This trip, we're quiet. I'm not the same person I was then. I'm thinking about how Lisa's tiny body is so compromised and now this. Mark is already talking lawsuit.

Two gastrointestinal doctors are waiting for us when we arrive at the Emergency Room.

Wednesday, December 1, 1982

Lisa has undergone CAT scans, ultrasounds and MRIs. After several conferences with the team of gastroenterologists, we meet with Dr. Gold.

He looks at Mark. "I've spoken with the surgeon and it appears the foreign object is the end of the drainage tube that broke off when it was pulled out after her Kasai."

"How could it have broken?" I ask.

"Sometimes it happens. We've questioned the intern who pulled the drain and they didn't notice anything unusual. That's why there's a radioactive isotope marker on any apparatus used during surgery in case of such of thing."

Mark leans forward. "When will they go in and get it?"

Dr. Gold clears his throat. "The pediatric surgeon is not willing to operate just to get the foreign object out. He's made that very clear."

"What does that mean?" Mark is taken aback.

Dr. Gold continues. "He'll perform a liver biopsy and while in there, he'll look around for the object in order to remove it."

"I hope that works," I say.

Dr. Gold shakes his head. "Unfortunately, since the surgery was almost a year ago, the amount of scar tissue that has developed will create poor visibility for him to locate the object."

I take a quick breath. *It's not over.*

"He'll do a thorough job and hopefully will find and remove the drainage tube."

Mark and I look at each other. He takes my hand.

Thursday, December 2, 1982

The surgeon is walking over to us, shaking his head. "I could not hunt around to find the drainage tube."

My heart sinks, and I lean against Mark. He himself is almost unable to stand.

"I would have put Lisa's life at risk if I did. The area around her original surgery has formed too much scar tissue which is very sinuous. It was difficult to perform the liver biopsy. I'm sorry, but I had to make the decision to leave things as they are."

As we watch him walk away, Mark and I stand stunned.

We go to Lisa's room. Robotically, I go to her, talking to her in a happy but hollow voice. "Hey, sweetie, how are you doing? Mommy and Daddy are right here."

She stares at us, grunts a sound, and then starts to cry.

I'm beyond angry or else so angry I don't even know it. They say when anger doesn't have an expression, it turns inward into depression. I feel incredibly sad. I'm remembering years of feeling alone as a child. There were days I would hide under my covers wishing for everyone I knew to go away. I'd hold my breath and count to 10 and then 20 to see if I could just stop living.

How am I going to survive this?

TOOLS

MEDICATION

WHEN THINGS ARE OUT OF CONTROL

Dr. Gold arrives at the recovery room and takes Mark and me to the conference room. "In light of our inability to remove the foreign object from your daughter's abdomen, we've come up with a plan that we believe will work to stop the recurrent fevers."

I'm hearing him speaking and yet, I'm struggling to comprehend what he's saying. I find myself starting to sink back into the Twilight Zone.

"We're going to discharge Lisa to your local hospital where she'll continue IV antibiotic therapy for a full two weeks. We want to keep her near your home." He gestures to both of us with visible compassion for the toll these last many months have taken on our family life. "Once the IV therapy is complete, we recommend six months of twice daily intra-muscular Gentamycin injections which should help Lisa's body wall off the foreign object."

I've never heard of such a thing. My mind is barely functioning.

He explains. "This will allow the formation of scar tissue around the object and it'll fool the body into thinking the object is gone. We've seen this happen before and feel there's a good chance the infections will stop. Of course, we're not a hundred percent sure the infections are caused by this foreign object or by her liver becoming compromised by the intestinal bacteria. Time will tell."

He sits back and waits for our reaction.

"Who's going to give the injections?" Mark asks.

"Well, your local hospital can set that up. It can either be the visiting nurse or one of you," he suggests.

"I can't give Lisa a shot," I say more loudly than called for. The thought of giving this tiny baby a shot makes me nauseous. I try to calm my voice. "I'm sorry, but I just can't."

Mark shakes his head as well.

"No problem. I understand," Dr. Gold says. "A nurse will come to your home twice a day. We want your lives to return to some form of normalcy. Your local hospital will make all the arrangements, and we've got some time to set this up since Lisa won't be going home for a few weeks." He stands and starts towards the door. "Hang in there. I'm confident this plan will work. But we have to stay calm. I'm going to ask for a psychiatric consult so you can get the necessary assistance to help deal with the ongoing stress." Dr. Gold exits with his team in tow.

I'm staring at the open door. We're supposed to walk out of the conference room and go back to our lives. Are drugs going to make this easier? What was it he said? Return to some form of normalcy. What is normalcy? Was the normalcy I felt this year a figment of my imagination? Lisa started to vocalize but has stopped. She doesn't crawl. There are endless infections. Every morning, I wake up wanting this to be over, and now I'm told my young daughter will live for the rest of her life with a foreign object inside her and that hopefully it will be walled off as if it isn't there. Like a moat around a castle—what, like Camelot disappearing into the mist?

WHAT I LEARNED

How do I believe anyone when they are talking to

me? Who is telling me the truth? How do I know that anything I feel is real?

Sometimes I just want to be completely alone so I can be with myself and no one else. Then I won't have to feel, see, and hear anyone.

Sometimes I don't want to be any more. Sometimes I don't want to be responsible for anyone or anything. I just want to be left alone so I can be miserable. But we have to survive in this world, struggling to make money to pay our bills so we don't lose everything.

It's like I have to think outside the box when the world wants to define the box I'm in. There's a tide of mass thought and unconsciousness. I feel my fight against it. I see only a world full of struggle, loss and suffering. How can we survive when it takes a lifetime to figure out how to manage in this system?

When an adult is diagnosed with a serious illness, we question whether the illness was brought on by negative thinking. I've read that our beliefs are part of a mind/body connection; it's a theory I still ponder to this day. But when a brand new baby comes into this world with a horrible illness, how can anyone make sense of this? Why do the innocent and helpless have to suffer?

Why is success defined by how much you own and what you look like? Why is noise so offensive to me? How can one so different fit into a world of look-a-likes? How come anything that comes from the heart has less value than something that comes from plastic or metal? How come we value our elderly less? How come so many people believe more is better?

This depression is hanging over my head exhausting me. I can't shake it; I can't go on living with it.

I go to a psychiatrist.

HOW IT HELPS

The psychiatrist hands me two prescriptions, one for an anti-depressant and the other for an anti-anxiety drug. "It'll help you ease some of these symptoms," he says. "You may find it easier to deal with your life. If you feel the drug is not helping, give me a call and we can talk about something else."

I stare at the pieces of paper. I'm remembering how dependent my father was on alcohol to live his life. I hated what it did to my family when I was a child. I don't want to use a substance that could hurt my own family now. *This is not going to turn me into my father. It's going to help me survive.*

Even with my sanity on the edge of reason, I know that I want to do this on life's terms. But at the moment, I cannot. I will remember this is just a tool, a temporary one. I want to be present for Michelle, for Lisa, and for Mark. There will be a time when I will be off these meds. I take the pills.

THERAPY

WHEN THINGS ARE OUT OF CONTROL

"How are you doing?" Dr. Kapher asks. We're at Lisa's weekly checkup.

"We're trying to adjust as best we can but it's hard. I worry about everything," I add, not going into details of how I stand over her crib wondering whether she'll die during her sleep. If it isn't that, then I'm wondering what will happen next. Will the Kasai stop working? Will Lisa turn yellow? I take a deep breath and unclench my jaw. "All I seem to do is cry. How do I know if something is wrong with her? I feel like I can't relax." The tears roll down my cheeks.

WHAT I LEARNED

"Are you seeing a therapist? You need to talk with one." Dr. Kapher smiles and places his hand on my shoulder.

"I'm on a waiting list."

"That just won't do." Dr. Kapher takes the telephone receiver off the wall and calls his assistant. "Nora, call downstairs to the Department of Mental Health and get them on the phone for me." He hangs up. "You need to speak to someone immediately." He turns to leave the room and then adds, "I'll see what I can do to get you an appointment."

Within 24 hours, I have my first appointment with a psychotherapist. Her name is Sarah.

Mark and I co-own a retail store in a mall five minutes from our home. Mark has a sales area but he also has an office in the back that is comfortable and private. It's a perfect place to leave Lisa while I go to my psychotherapy appointment.

Sarah is an older woman, with salt and pepper hair and a warm smile. She gestures to me to take a seat.

I start in. "Basically, I'm falling apart trying to deal with my new baby. I don't know what to do with all my feelings. I'm scared to death something is going to happen to her. I don't seem to care much about anything and I have a three-year-old daughter who I need to care for as well." My hands are shaking. My stomach is doing somersaults and my knees are trembling.

Sarah is supportive. I feel like someone is finally hearing me.

I recount the interaction I had while I was waiting in the doctor's office, how that woman said she couldn't deal with my story. The pain on Sarah's face is obvious as she listens.

"I'm never telling anyone again," I blurt out. "I can't believe how that woman stopped me mid-sentence." Tears are pouring down my face. "Does she have any idea how hard it was to even say what I said?"

"You're in a very vulnerable place," Sarah reminds me. "It's important for you to protect yourself and not share from such a hurt place unless you can trust who you're talking to. You need to practice discernment with anyone you speak with."

This lesson is a revelation to me. I don't have to share my whole story with everyone who's asking me how I am. I get to decide whether a person is safe. I get to choose what I share and who I share it with. The painful interaction with that woman served as a lesson teaching me the importance of strong boundaries in public. Boundaries are not something I learned from my family when I was a child. I never questioned the rules I learned.

But I can question them. Sarah is giving me permission. She helps me create a script for when people ask me how I am or how things are going.

HOW IT HELPS

Having a script helps me respond. If it's an acquaintance, I say I'm not in a space to share or else I say I'm okay. If they inquire about the new baby, I say there have been some complications, but nothing I wish to share right now. If it's a friend who's really asking, I update them while keeping aware of how deeply I want to share. I check in with myself regarding my sense of safety and how much I trust this person. I'm making my boundaries explicit and I'm sticking to them. I'm throwing away my old rules and beginning to build new rules for communicating with people so I can protect myself from emotional upset.

When people say, "Hi, how are you?" they aren't really expecting a real response. So I've given myself permission to ignore their question and just move on to the next step in the conversation. People never notice!

JOURNALING

WHEN THINGS ARE OUT OF CONTROL

Lisa's intramuscular antibiotic injections are administered at 8:00 a.m. and 4:30 p.m. Our visiting nurse's name is Merissa. After a few days, Lisa figures out what Merissa is here for and starts wailing as soon as she comes in the door.

After today's injection, I hold Lisa and rock her to quiet her. Then I put her down on the floor and bring out her favorite music board to play with. She rolls over to the couch and pulls herself up. Leaning on the couch, she walks to her favorite stuffed bunny and laughs.

Every time Merissa walks in the door to give Lisa her injection, the incessant crying is almost intolerable. I want to scream.

I find it painful to run into people I know so I'm staying isolated from any unnecessary contact with the public.

I try hard to get some sort of routine going. Every other week Lisa has an appointment with Dr. Kapher. Michelle needs my attention. Lisa cries from the pain.

And there's my own inner screaming. It's not something I acknowledge. The children would never understand, neither does Mark. It's been continuous as I fall further and further into the Twilight Zone. I'm exhausted, feeling helpless and lost not knowing what's the right answer.

WHAT I LEARNED

Sarah picks up her appointment book and holds it as if it were a journal. "Writing down your thoughts and feelings is very powerful, cathartic and helps deal with the anxiety and tension. Journaling gives you an outlet for all your thoughts. A journal can become your friend, your confidante that no one else needs to read. It will give you insight and room to feel your feelings. I really recommend you think about creating a journal for yourself." She smiles and sits forward in her chair.

That night, I try journaling.

For as long as I can remember, food has been my friend. Food has lessened the emotional pain, distracted me from my life and created a sense of safety for me. Overeating helps me numb my inner pain.

Do not take the food out of my mouth
For it helps me be brave
My mouth is full and my belly is safe
My mind is busy with my belly busy

I do not feel when my belly is full
I do not sense when my mouth is busy

Am I able to take steps beyond my full stomach?
My safety relies on meals
My steps into my new world are imprinted on buttered bread

How much clearer will I hear if my stomach is growling?
What does it mean to me to be hungry?

****

We lived next to a blueberry farm with dirt paths between the fields. As a young adolescent, I remember saddling up an imaginary horse and spending hours walking and running with my imaginary friend in the fields.

I finally got a horse when I was 15. Betsy was a Morgan mare, beautiful dark brown coat with black mane and tail. We had a corral on the side of our property where I would ride Betsy putting her through her paces. I rode English. I created games for us to play, leaving my crop on the low roof of the hay shed and grabbing it as I trotted or cantered by.

One summer, we went on a 10-day family trip. Betsy stayed at a nearby farm. When we returned, Betsy was lame. The vet said she had laminitis which happens when horses get overheated and eat green grass and drink too much cold water. It turned into a yearlong illness which never got better. I remember sleeping in her stall leaning on her as she laid on her side. My riding days were over.

One day, I came home from school to discover that my parents had had her euthanized. I was shattered. My best friend was dead and I had no opportunity to say goodbye, no preparation, no respect for what I needed, no honoring of the deep friendship we had.

I vowed on that day I would never get my hopes up again over anything and to hate my parents for the rest of my life.

HOW IT HELPS

Personally, I hate to journal. It feels like a waste of time. My critic screams for complete sentences and I want to proofread everything. But in my journal, I write my resistance down, pushing past my impatience. All my complaints have their say. I give all the yuck some air.

Then the real stuff comes out—how I'm really feeling. The critic is a hump in the road: the goal is to get past the critic road block. Move through it and then you've got space in your journal to emote and purge all you want. It works if you work it.

May my tears heal my broken parts. May they fill my empty inner pain and may they find my voice as I struggle to express my needs and desires.

May my tears wash out the old pages and bring new words and meaning to my life. May the true me be revealed so that I may find inner happiness and learn to live again.

STRESS-RELIEVING TECHNIQUES

WHEN THINGS ARE OUT OF CONTROL

Lisa is nearing her six-month deadline for the intramuscular injections. The injection therapy is working. I've gotten into a daily routine and find myself out in public more often.

This afternoon, it's particularly busy at the grocery store. I hear a child crying the next aisle over. I stop in my tracks.

I run my hand over my forehead and I'm sweating. My hands become clammy. My head starts to hurt and suddenly, I can't breathe. My ears feel like they're blocked and I realize I need to get out of this store right now.

I leave my full cart and run out. I'm doubled over in the parking lot pressed against my car trying to catch my breath. The world is spinning.

After about 15 minutes, I'm able to get in the car and drive home, sobbing all the way. I feel like I'm back at square one.

WHAT I LEARNED

My therapist tells me this was a panic attack. A crying child triggered me. After all I have been through, it's understandable.

I ask her how do I deal with panic attacks. She says that every panic attack is manageable if it's caught. The key is becoming aware at the beginning of the panic and catching it before it gets out of hand.

There are techniques that can relieve the immediate stress by changing one's focus.

When I feel a panic attack coming on, I can hold a coin in one hand and pass it to the other hand over and over again. This repetitive coin-manipulating technique helps focus the brain, taking one's attention away from the feeling of panic.

Another technique is square breathing. Sarah says, "Breathe in to the count of four. Hold to the count of four. Breathe out to the count of four. Hold to the count of four." She walks me through several rounds and I feel calmness and slowing of my whole being. It takes just a matter of a few minutes and the result is immediate.

HOW IT HELPS

Sitting in therapy, I pass the coin between my hands. It occurs to me that people fiddle with their fingers all the time. "I can do this without anybody noticing it either."

I was in the grocery store this morning. While I stood in the checkout line, I passed a quarter between my hands. I felt the comfort of it. It's a tool I literally keep in my pocket.

If I stick to the places I'm used to going, I have less anxiety. The minute I do something different, I feel a panic attack coming on. I had to go to the Registry of Motor Vehicles to renew my license. *Breathe in, hold, breathe out, hold.* I kept square breathing the whole time. It kept my panic attack in check.

STAYING IN THE PRESENT

WHEN THINGS ARE OUT OF CONTROL

When Lisa was diagnosed with a chronic illness, every other responsibility in our lives fell by the wayside and was labeled as non-important. How do I find peace and relaxation again? Sometimes when I try writing, I write in circles and get lost because my emotions overtake me.

If I were to picture what I looked like in the hospital with Lisa when she was first diagnosed, my eyes were wide like saucers. I wore the same clothes every day. A grimace of emotional pain etched my forehead and reshaped my mouth as I cried. I was polite to the nurses, doctors, other parents, and caregivers surrounding us, but with Mark, I cried. We ate because we had to. We slept because we were exhausted. And every day, we awoke to the horror of sick kids everywhere from all over the world. I looked with unbelieving eyes at the room full of cribs finding the one with Lisa in it, our Lisa.

I try to mother her the way I mothered Michelle, but nothing is the same. This huge scar wraps around her little belly from side to side. It's like she's cut in half, looking like Bert's mouth on Sesame Street. If it weren't for the stitches holding her together, it would gape open like the Muppets do. Oh, Michelle laughs so much at the Muppets. But Lisa's belly would fall open and drain the life out of her.

Impending doom hangs over our family with this sick child. Birthday parties, preschool, baby clothes, toys, everything that suggests happiness threatens me.

Michelle is a delight and reminds me what healthy means. My focus is all outward helping, nourishing, cleaning, whatever moms do.

But I've built fortress walls to protect myself. It keeps my emotions on hold because if I were to feel them, they would kill me. Focusing outward is safe as I take care of Michelle and Lisa. When I'm alone with Mark, there's nothing but tears and I start over every morning to begin again.

My worry and emotional rawness goes everywhere with me. I feel so lost. In therapy, I talk of the horrors of Lisa's disease and all the "what-could-happens." I glance at Sarah's face which is grimaced in like mine is. This brand new baby is broken, stuttering to life and only living because of the surgery they did that cut her in half.

I'm so scared going outside of the house. I can't remember in the moment to use the tools Sarah taught me. I get used to having panic attacks which grab my throat and choke me. My breath suddenly becomes tighter and tighter and I gasp without realizing what's happening. Pressure pushes on the sides of my eyes and my ears like I'm going to faint. I feel like I'm hanging on for dear life. The world is teeming around me while my baby is living and dying. I feel like I'm losing my mind.

Sarah tells me I suffer from agoraphobia. I have to muster a tremendous courage to do any kind of mundane errand outside the home. I have to scope out my moves to get to my destinations. Anything throws me off and I have to go home. Sometimes I feel like I'm in a war zone.

Something happens to me when I don't do what I'm expecting of myself. I start blaming myself for all the wrongs. Even when I write. I get tangled in the emotions and so lost in the feelings, I lose my way.

WHAT I LEARNED

I'm holding all the pain from the past—with everything that's happened to Lisa, all the emotional upheaval of her birth, surgery, diagnosis, and struggle to fit into a world where no one wants to hear about a sick baby. I carry that with me in everything I do. At the same time, I worry whether she will live. I worry that she'll become immune to the drugs. I worry about all the what-ifs that may occur. I worry about her future. I am so preoccupied with the past and the future that I'm not paying attention to the present. So where am I, really?

Day after day, I sit in this puddle of worry and concern. The truth is I'm right here and right now. I'm not in the future and I'm not in the past. If I can keep my thoughts of the past and the worries about the future out of my head, I will be living in the present. It's my fear that bulldozes me into feeling immobile and exhausted.

I need something really simple, a gesture, anything to remind myself this is where I am right now—I'm not back then and I'm not jumping ahead. What could it be?

I touch my nose. I can touch my nose. By casually touching my nose, I'm reminded I am here. I am now. If I do this simple gesture in public, no one will notice. After all, I rub my nose if I have a tickle. I hold my nose if I have to sneeze.

Every time I touch my nose, it will remind me the time is now.

HOW IT HELPS

Lisa wakes from her nap. I walk in and smile at her. Immediately, my mind catapults back to the endless array of cribs she's lain in at Boston Children's Hospital. I realize what I'm doing and catch myself.

I touch my nose. I'm back to the present. I pick her up and hug her. She's here now and so am I. That's all I know. Nothing else matters. We have a close moment as I love her. I'm so glad I'm present.

Years later, when I talk with another therapist, I tell him about touching my nose. He laughs. "That's a good one. I jangle my keys in my pocket, and it helps me remember I'm an adult."

ASSERTIVENESS TRAINING

WHEN THINGS ARE OUT OF CONTROL

I speak to my mother every few days on the phone. Our communication is a struggle. She doesn't listen to what I'm saying.

"Well, think about it this way," she says. "It could be worse and Lisa could have died."

Am I supposed to feel better by that comment? I hang up from our conversations feeling even emptier. Neither she nor my father even suggested coming into Boston to support me. And they're not that far away either, only two hours.

Lisa is all right at the moment with monthly checkups that are all positive as a result of the injections.

But I'm remembering the days walking the hospital halls with Lisa to stop her from crying. I would talk to other mothers and fathers about their children, asking what their child is in for. I looked for another family with a serious situation so I could connect with someone who knows what I'm feeling, but most families were in for short stays.

Lisa's blood was tested daily. Sometimes the doctors wouldn't let me into the treatment rooms, so I had to wait in the hall. When she was taken from me, I would pace up and down waiting for it to be over but I couldn't get away from her hysterical screaming. On other occasions, I was allowed in the treatment rooms to help hold her down. I'm told she's a tough draw. Her little veins collapse, roll and just plain disappear, so taking blood becomes a daily challenge. What an odd way to get to know one's child—by the behavior of her veins.

There were—and are—so many doctors' questions, opinions and choices to make, choices that may work or not. My head spins with it all.

I do not know how to make decisions, and I'm scared to make ones that might lead down a road of no return. I feel immobilized.

WHAT I LEARNED

I can't spend the rest of my life in hiding. I find a course on assertiveness training at a local college. The workshop is going to be held for three hours once a week for four weeks.

Tonight is the first night of my assertiveness training. The teacher Jim says that role playing is going to be a big part in the class. I'm not sure I can do this, but I made this commitment to myself to do something or else I will go crazy. I can't keep hiding.

Jim asks us about our decision-making process. I tell him I don't know what I want.

He says, "Let's pick something easy. Like buying a pair of shoes. How do you pick a pair of shoes?"

"I don't know." I'm glancing to the door wondering if I could just disappear.

"Okay." He opens a box with two shoes in it. "Which of these do you prefer?"

I look down and pick the one on the right. "I like this one."

"Why?"

"I like the strap on it."

"See? You have a preference. That's part of the decision-making process, learning to believe in your preferences."

This is the second night of the assertiveness training workshop. Jim talks more about decisions. We go through piles of shoes until we each have the shoe we like. As we stare at our picks, he talks about teasing a decision apart. "It's like a spinning wheel that looks like one color. When you slow it down, you can see the individual colors." He has a broad smile.

I'm thinking of it more like strands hanging from floating balloons. I can grab at one and examine it in order to see what it's all about.

We do more role-playing. I find that I like it. It's giving me tools to find my voice.

It's the third week. The scenes we participate in are more challenging than choosing a pair of shoes. I play a role where I'm an employee who's been late to work. My boss is trying to intimidate me. I practice maintaining eye contact. I know that in the past, I would have put up with his threats; I would have over-apologized and withdrawn. Instead, I hear myself being honest and concise about my feelings.

I go to the fourth and last class. As I listen to the workshop leader, I realize that there are different types of intimidation. This training is helping me stand up to doctors, but it isn't helping me deal with a sick child.

HOW IT HELPS

I'm pacing the room. We've been in the hospital for a two-day test. We're waiting for discharge papers, wanting to get out and home. We're all exhausted. I'm sure Lisa feels like a pin cushion.

In walks a young male doctor. "We'd like to take one last X-ray before you leave," he says. "I've got papers here and all you need to do is sign your permission." He shuffles the papers before us.

"Why this X-ray? Dr. Gold didn't mention this to me."

He mumbles something about "research."

That gets my attention. "No, sorry, that won't happen here." I walk him towards the door.

The doctor is surprised. "Are you sure? It won't take long and it will aid in further research of liver disease."

"Nope, sorry. It's not going to happen." I try not to slam the door shut on him.

Energized by the assertiveness training, I decide to develop a plan. I'm going to build a toolkit and do research to educate myself. To be forewarned is to be forearmed. I'm going to write down questions for the next doctor's appointment. And to be sure to ask questions of a trusted doctor in the medical specialty. Everyone has an opinion and some opinions are better not shared. I'm only going to listen to trusted sources.

SUPPORT GROUP

WHEN THINGS ARE OUT OF CONTROL

It's Lisa's second birthday. We celebrate with chocolate cake and vanilla ice cream. I play the organ. Lisa stands on the couch rocking her little off-centered body back and forth and yelling, "Eh, eh." Michelle dances on the floor twirling in circles.

For a brief moment, I feel normal. I also know deep down it's an illusion.

At her monthly checkup, Dr. Kapher wants to discuss Lisa's development. I tell him about my concern with her lack of mobility. "She can get around in her baby walker or holding furniture but something doesn't seem right," I explain.

"Does she crawl?"

"She never did."

"She never did?"

"No. She tries to keep up with Michelle but doesn't have the mobility. If someone or something gets too close to her body, she flails her arms in self-defense."

Dr. Kapher pulls out some forms. "Let's start her on occupational and physical therapy."

I'm so angry. I'm going through this hell and I feel so alone. There must be other people going through this. Why must I do this alone and have no one to talk to? I heard there's a support group in Boston, but that's two hours away. It's bad enough we have to drive there to go to the hospital. There's no way I can justify going there for myself. Perhaps I can start a support group for other parents. Why not help each other?

At Lisa's next monthly checkup with Dr. Kapher, I take a deep breath and try to remember what I learned at the assertiveness training. "I want to start a support group for parents of chronically-ill children. Parents need to talk with other parents who understand what they're going through."

Dr. Kapher looks over my written proposal. "This is a good idea. You're right, there's certainly a need for parents to talk with each other."

"Would you be able to help me start this?" I hold my breath.

"Sure. We can post a flyer of your support group in our office."

I'm smiling as I leave. What I didn't tell him was the reason I need to do this. Maybe this way I won't feel so alone. Truthfully, if I don't do something, I don't think I will survive.

WHAT I LEARNED

My support group has a name! I call it "A Mother's Heart Connection." I've had the sign posted in Dr. Kapher's office for a month now and I've received calls from several parents.

A Mother's Heart Connection officially meets tonight. Carol, one of the moms, offered her house. Five families are involved, some of the fathers are present. Mark works on Friday nights, so I hire a babysitter who lives only a few minutes away. The group has a good talk. Everyone says the same thing, it's nice to talk with other parents. I can see the visible relief on their faces. I must look the same.

Our support group meets again at Carol's house. Five mothers and one father show up. We all have so much pain over our children. It's so sad. We're still uncertain with each other, each of us so burdened by our lives. But I do find that something about the sharing helps.

Six families show up for the third support group meeting. I'm excited. It's a good group. People are commenting how helpful it is.

One would think that hearing about other people's pain would be a burden, but it's not. I feel the pain in their stories and I wish I could make it all go away. It's like we're transferring a piece of our own private hells onto each other. But the transferred pain isn't so heavy and it makes our own burden a bit lighter. It's like we're knitting ourselves together into this web. We even smile afterwards.

I look forward to our next group session.

It's Friday night and the support group is meeting again. I'm becoming friendly with some of the moms in the group.

It's my turn to share. "I do what I have to do," I say, explaining how I make my life work with Mark working so much.

"How do you deal with hiring babysitters all the time?" a father asks.

"What choice do I have? It's a juggling act." I answer. "Last week, both kids were sound asleep so I just drove the babysitter home and was back home within six minutes."

"What do you mean you left your kids sleeping?" one father bellows. "You left your kids alone? That's inexcusable." The father slams his hands on his thighs and stands up exasperated. "Do you know what could happen when you leave your kids alone?"

I don't know what to say. I would not ever put my children in harm's way. What choice did I have?

The man's wife injects, "Calm down, Jerry. We all do the best we can."

But he continues. "I can't believe you work so hard to help your child live and then you abandon her without her even knowing it in her sleep. You're off your rocker, lady!" Jerry storms out of the room.

I look at the other mothers in disbelief. I can't help myself and I start to cry. "I didn't do anything wrong. They were fine," I say as I walk into the kitchen. I can hear Jerry in the other room yelling at his wife. The tears just keep rolling down my face.

Carol follows me to comfort me.

My assertiveness training has gone out the window. "I feel like I committed murder or something. What am I supposed to do? Mark works all the time and I need to get out."

I hear the front door slam.

"What happened?" I ask Carol to check. "I'm not going out there again."

She returns. "That was Jerry's method of exiting. His wife was crying as they left," she adds. "There's got to be something wrong with him the way he went ballistic on you. I would have done the same thing as you did. You didn't do anything wrong," she repeats, trying to comfort me.

Robotically, we clean up the food. The moms chat amongst themselves but the whole encounter leaves a terrible taste in everyone's mouth.

The Mother's Heart Connection support group is disbanding. Maybe broken people can't be together in one space without having a trained leader to guide them. Did I expect too much of us? I can't accept being judged for my actions. I'm doing the best I can in an impossible situation. I hardly get support for what I'm doing, and now my one attempt at sharing this burden has collapsed.

HOW IT HELPS

Years later, I start another support group called "Our Care" for parents and caregivers of chronically-ill and special needs children. Our local hospital provides me with support from a pediatric social worker. With the professional guidance, we do much better. A hard lesson learned.

Last week, I was in a small shopping center and was walking from a parking garage to the stores. Approaching on the walk ramp was an elderly woman fussing over a differently-abled son, helping him with his jacket, encouraging him to have a good time.

As the simple moment passed, this mother and son brought to mind a truth about parents and caregivers. No matter the age of the child—baby through adulthood—a mom is always a mom and a dad is always a dad. We help our children the best we can. We have heartache at any age for their chronic illness or disability. And it comes down to *our care* in the process of our caring for them. We are the foundation upon which our children survive. It is our gift to them from our humaneness and love. And as long as we take care and love them, we need care as well.

COMMUNITY

WHEN THINGS ARE OUT OF CONTROL

It's Thanksgiving. We spend the day at Mark's mom's house about an hour away. It's what we normally do, at least what we normally did before Lisa was born.

The dinner goes fine. Any day is easier when there are other adults around helping. We all notice how Lisa's eyelids flutter when she tries to speak and her arms become rigid.

Mark's mother remarks on it. "It sounds like she is stuttering."

Every muscle in me tightens; it's like everyone is pointing their fingers at me. I birthed a sick child, a child that could barely learn to walk. And now that child cannot even learn to talk.

"I want to talk to you about Lisa's speech," Laverne, the daycare teacher, says, pulling me aside. Lisa is climbing up a play structure. "Her word usage seems to be diminishing rather than increasing."

"What do you suggest I do?"

"Talk to her pediatrician about our concern. He'll know what direction to take."

I can feel the panic start. My mind is racing everywhere at once. What if there is something else wrong? I don't know what I'll do. But a small thread in the middle of the enlarging ideas floats past me, and I bring my finger near my nose and lightly touch it. "I'll call him today."

Dr. Kapher asks me what I notice about Lisa's speech.

"She's getting stuck saying words. She'll point and grunt more than speak."

"Toddlers should be saying maybe 100 words."

"She's nowhere near that. Will she grow out of the stuttering?"

"Some do. We'll start her on speech therapy."

"So young?" I ask.

"Yes."

Lisa is to start speech therapy once a week. First, a child psychologist conducts tests on her. She is then referred to a pediatric neurologist to investigate possible seizure activity.

Our speech therapist, Bill, travels with us to Boston Children's Hospital where a study is performed. Lisa is hooked up to an EEG monitor. She has wires all over her head.

Lisa sits on a stretcher and Bill talks to her encouraging her to use her words. Up on the wall are two screens. The left one is Lisa unaware she's on camera. The camera is focused in on her face as she talks. The other screen depicts the EEG monitor with its wave patterns changing and arcing as she speaks.

"Her brain waves are certainly peculiar," Dr. Pearson says. "It's unclear whether she's having a seizure as she speaks."

There's more than fifteen on the team of neurologists and student interns crammed into the conference room. It's an unusual study to them. To me, it's my life. I step back from it all for a moment and notice the peaked interest of the doctors. This is all about my daughter, Lisa. I just stand there watching.

Inside, I am crying.

"I'm attending a national conference on pediatric neurology in Tucson next week," Dr. Pearson says. "I'd like to present Lisa's case. Her brain wave patterns are peculiar and I would like to get other specialists' opinions." His eyes are lit up. "This is a great opportunity for the country's experts to put their heads together."

I nod my consent.

He pauses. "I'll give you a call the week after next with the suggestions we come up with."

Dr. Pearson is on the phone. "The consensus is Lisa has unusual brain wave patterns. It's unclear whether they're seizure related, so this is my recommendation. To rule out whether it's seizure activity, I'd like to start her on a trial of Tegretol."

I'm hating this word 'seizure'. When it came up originally, I didn't want to give credence to the possibility of it being real. Now, he's recommending a drug for it.

Dr. Pearson continues. "Tegretol is an anti-seizure medication. If in fact these are seizures," he says, "there will be an improvement in her speech patterns."

"You think she's having seizures as she talks?" I ask.

"Well, it's a possibility we have to rule out," he answers. "I'll call her speech therapist and tell him what I want him to look for as he's working with her. We'll start her on the lowest dose possible and go from there."

Oh, heavens, another drug. She's already taking a pharmacy's inventory.

"One of the side effects to this drug is it can lower

her platelet count if the dosage is too high. So once Lisa is at a therapeutic level, she'll need a blood test to monitor her levels."

She's been on the Tegretol a week. The good news is there is no change in Lisa's speech pattern. This means she's not having seizures. The bad news is she continues to struggle with her words and she's extremely frustrated.

"This is Dr. Thornton from Health Services," the man's voice says on the phone. "Are you Lisa's mom?"

"Yes." I'm not sure what to expect from this phone call.

"It's important that you hear what I have to say. Lisa's platelet count has become so low she's considered a bleeder," he says. "What is she doing right now?"

"She's playing on the floor in the living room." My eyes widen. "Why?"

"I don't want to alarm you," he hesitates, "but it's very important that you don't give Lisa any more Tegretol for the next 24 hours. And make sure she doesn't fall or bump herself in any way."

My eyes widen further as I brush my nose. "She's a toddler and you're asking me to stop her from running or playing?"

"It's important that she doesn't hurt herself," he says. "Twenty-four hours should be enough time for her platelets to stabilize and then you don't have to worry about it."

"So what you're saying is the trial of Tegretol failed because of her reaction to it?"

"Well, it's obvious this isn't the answer. Dr.

Pearson will be in touch with you for the next steps. I felt it was important to get in touch with you right away." He hangs up.

I go into the living room, trying to figure out how I'm going to watch Lisa for the next 24 hours. She loves to be active. I feel hopeless. What next is going to go wrong? I'm hanging onto a thread with therapy. Mark doesn't understand what I'm going through and doesn't believe therapy is helpful. The kids can't comprehend what's happening. My parents pretend nothing is wrong.

I sit down next to Lisa and pull out a book. I start to read it to her but my mind is racing. The anti-depressant and anti-anxiety pills I've been on for almost a year now have helped, but I want to find an alternative solution.

The story I'm reading her is about a little girl visiting all the people in her town. On one of the pages is a church with a big white steeple and smiling families in front of it.

Why not try going to a church again? I had tried the year after Lisa was born but some scandal around the minister left me disappointed. Should I try another church?

I feed Lisa lunch, talking all through it. Thankfully, she takes a short nap. Somehow, we make it through the day.

WHAT I LEARNED

Feeling brave, I go to The Church of Life, a United Church of Christ community right in town. I love the service. It's full of music and inspiration. It holds my attention. There's something about community and common purpose in a church that I respond to. But it has to be full of spirit, acceptance, and peace. With a name like The Church of Life, it could be the type of church I've been hoping for.

The Church of Life continues to fulfill me. It's fun and I love to sing. The pastor, Jason, is a gay man. His partner, Johnny, is the musical director. The Church of Life is forming a choir. Auditions are next Sunday after services. I'm thinking about joining. They say I can sing any song.

I sing 'Happy Birthday.' I pass the audition and officially join the Voices of Life Choir.

In church this morning, the congregation sings 'Happy Birthday' to me. I'll be 33 years old tomorrow. I feel close to the minister and the congregation. I feel hopeful when I'm here. Singing makes me feel happy. The choir is having a concert in mid-May. I invite Mark and the girls.

The choir concert is this afternoon. "Are you coming to the concert with us?" I'm packing snacks and look at Mark.

"Do I have to? You know I don't like churches. I was going to go work on my boat," Mark says, trying to sidle out the door.

"It's not about a church. It's about being together as a family." I shove the milk container into the refrigerator and slam the door shut.

Michelle looks at Mark who looks at her and then me.

"Oh, all right."

Why is it so hard to get Mark to do anything with me? I feel so happy when I sing.

HOW IT HELPS

Sometimes I bring the girls to The Church of Life. Almost every Sunday, I sing in the choir. I find that when I sing, I'm only hearing my voice. For those few minutes, I am me, I hear me, and I am at peace.

I'm an alto. The choir members have become my family. When I'm singing, I focus on feeling good. I sing in the shower. I sing to my girls. I found this wonderful song called *Everything Possible* by Fred Small. He talks about being who you want to be, that the measure of a person is the love you leave behind.

I ask Michelle and Lisa if I can sing the song to them before bed.

They roll their eyes. "Okay." It's like they're putting up with me.

It means so much to me to say and sing these words to them. I feel such love for them. I can see in their eyes they're feeling it too.

COURAGE TO ASK FOR HELP

WHEN THINGS ARE OUT OF CONTROL

Mark left for work at 8:30 this morning. Mall hours are pretty brutal. He'll be there until 10:00 tonight. Lisa and Michelle have eaten their breakfast. Lisa's words are coming better these days, but she has become more aggressive.

I can hear Michelle shrieking, "Give me it!"

"No!" Lisa yells. I can hear the fast shuffling of feet as Michelle chases after Lisa. I pop my head around the corner and see Lisa strike Michelle in the face.

Michelle wails, "Mommy, Lisa hit me." She takes a breath and screams louder, holding her hand over her left eye. "It hurts."

I bend down and take away the toy that caused the fight. Then I turn and pick Michelle up, sit down and place her on my lap.

"Let me look at your eye, honey."

"It hurts," she cries. Her eye is shut tight and tears are streaming from it.

I hold her for a while but she can't open her eye. Lisa starts crying herself. I reach over and hold her and realize she's hot. *Oh heavens, she has a fever.*

I call Mark and tell him what happened with Michelle.

"She might have a scratch on her cornea," Mark says. "Call Health Services and see if you can go in even though it's Saturday."

"Can you watch Lisa at the store?" I ask. "I can drop her off and bring some food and some toys."

"Yeah, okay," he says. "I'll do my best. I hope it

doesn't get busy."

"I don't think she feels good. She's a little hot but she has a runny nose. Let's hope it's just a cold."

"Michelle's got a scratch on her cornea," the doctor says. "The dye confirms the scratch. I can see it under the black light," he sits back. "She's going to need to wear a patch on her eye for a few days until it heals. Some Tylenol will help with the pain." He writes out the directions. "How did this happen?"

"Her sister hit her right in the eye." It's embarrassing. A three-year-old striking her older sister hard enough to hurt her.

I call Dr. Kapher. "Lisa has had a fever for two days and it's not going away. She's pretty miserable."

He orders the usual blood work and chest X-ray. What I've feared has come true. Her liver function tests are elevated. We're off to Boston for 10 days. Michelle is sent to her grandmother's, complete with one eye patch.

WHAT I LEARNED

I've been attempting to normalize my life in an abnormal situation. I've been trying to keep everything working—meals on the table, food in the house, Michelle dressed and going to kindergarten. Keep the house as clean as possible. Help Lisa thrive with all her appointments and meds and frustrations. Make my marriage work. Visit our parents so they can know the children. Create a normal life like everyone else has.

I can't control this anymore. I give up trying. There's no normal anything and I have to remember that. I have to ask for help.

HOW IT HELPED

Sometimes life just doesn't stop for us to take a breath. I decide to lean on friends and family, anyone I feel I can trust. I try reaching out to Mark's sisters.

"Of course," his younger sister says. "I'll come over and watch the kids your next big shopping trip."

I call my neighbor. She has a daughter named Annie. "Can I send Michelle over for a couple of hours? I have to take Lisa to the doctor's."

"Sure, we're designing Halloween costumes. I'll figure out costumes for your girls too."

"How'd you know I didn't have a plan yet?"

"Michelle will love the princess costume I've got in mind."

"Thanks." I grab Lisa up and tell Michelle to get ready.

Another time, I drive up to my house and see all these paper bags on the porch. Examining them, I see a three-course meal packed into containers. It's from a mother in Michelle's play group.

It's okay to ask for help, okay to not be the strongest rock in the room. If anyone other than my children depends on me in any way, shape or form, they're on their own. It's sink or swim.

However, I'm a people pleaser and caretaker, and I have to struggle to break the dynamic of dependence that I create in order to feel safe. A new friend needed me to pick her up because her car broke down. I told her we're heading out to the ER. I wanted to apologize but said instead, this is my life. I never heard from her again.

ACCEPTANCE VS DENIAL

WHEN THINGS ARE OUT OF CONTROL

I don't care what the doctors say; I'm going to find a cure. Modern medicine has cures for everything. People are surviving cancer when years ago they would have died. Paraplegics are walking on state-of-the-art limbs. People are surviving heart transplants; others are walking on the moon. What's one baby's liver?

After the first operation in December of 1981, my hopes were up. But the repetitive infections began occurring and it became clear that the surgery didn't solve everything. When they walled off the foreign object in her abdomen a year later, there was hope again. Lisa was fever-free for 18 months. But during that time, her problems with speech emerged. We started her on speech therapy. When the infections began again, the doctors had antibiotics. They always have more and more antibiotics. But the infections don't stop.

People suggest trying alternative solutions. I go to a body-worker for my own stress because I'm having trouble getting my health back. In the course of treatment, she suggests we take Lisa to the Center of Light healing circle in Western Massachusetts. I call them. Frances Smith, the main healer, suggests an extended treatment for Lisa.

Every Friday for six weeks, we drive an hour to the center. Seven women healers participate in a hands-on healing. We sit in a spiral on the floor; I'm in the middle with Lisa, and a healer alternates with members of the family including Mark and my mother. Frances, a woman in her 50's, sits on the outside and she concentrates on Lisa, sending healing energy through the spiral. The quiet praying feels so comfortable. At times, one or more women begin soft chanting. Lisa sleeps soundly through each hour session, her cheeks red.

At the third session, Frances speaks haltingly with eyes closed from in a deep trance and she starts describing the blockage. She's so intensely into it that she's sweating. After about 10 minutes, she opens her eyes and with a deep breath says, "There it goes." Frances has broken through the blockage. My face lights up with excitement and relief.

When I get home from each session, I put Lisa into her crib and stare at her, trying to determine if there's any improvement. After the six weeks are up, Frances wishes us well and says it's God's will.

We go on with our lives. Every three months, we are at Boston Children's Hospital for a checkup and blood work.

The infections don't stop.

Early on, the doctors started Lisa on supplements and vitamins. There are vitamin E, K and lots of other things. All to help her liver. Eventually, she's taken off the vitamins and supplements because she's doing better. It sounds so positive. It looks like she's getting better and maybe all the doctors' visits aren't necessary.

But the infections don't stop.

There is the gem therapy. Round discs with gemstones aiding liver function are laid on her for about 10 minutes at a time. I hold her with them on her. I'm hopeful it will help, but when it doesn't seem to be doing anything after a few sessions, we stop.

There is sound therapy by an English therapist. A tall, skinny man, Mr. Earle, explains that surgery cuts the energy body. He says physical healing can't occur until the energy body is mended. Hitting a tuning fork to make it vibrate, he holds it over Lisa's scar. We're given one so that I can do it at home.

But the infections don't stop.

There's the hands-on healing by a priest. We go to a huge church and sit with thousands of people. The choir sings on the stage accompanied by organ music. This raises the energy in the church. We spend the whole day with other families as the priest walks amongst us offering prayer and inspiration. We sit hoping the priest will come by with his healing touch. When he does, I hold Lisa up to him.

I don't notice any difference and the infections don't stop.

At the beginning of Lisa's speech therapy, the speech therapist asks me about a hundred different questions and looks pained as I tell the story of Lisa's birth and the subsequent events.

He plays with Lisa while I watch. He gives me some fun exercises to do with her using words to encourage her to speak.

Lisa's preschool teacher, Sheila, talks to me about what she's noticed. "Lisa has problems with comprehension and auditory processing. When she's given instructions to do things, she can't do them in the order they're given. She also doesn't seem to

TOOLS FOR THE EXCEPTIONAL PARENT

understand some simple instructions." Sheila suggests that over the summer, Lisa may need to work on understanding sequencing.

"I don't understand."

Sheila shows me pictures. "Getting ready for bed involves several steps: changing into pajamas, washing up, brushing your teeth, getting into bed. Lisa doesn't understand the order she would follow in that kind of situation."

I stare at the pictures. She recommends someone to help.

I meet with Elizabeth who practices the Tomatis Method of therapy for dealing with learning disabilities. Tomatis believes children born in a trauma experience overcome their auditory processing difficulties more easily by hemispheric integration. It's for cognitive understanding and sequencing. The tools he developed involve an electronic listening device that Lisa will wear.

Elizabeth records my voice as I recite a book of nursery rhymes. Then she filters the recording to a decibel level that a fetus would hear within the womb. This recording will play in Lisa's ears as she does play therapy with Elizabeth.

We go every Wednesday for an hour and a half, and I watch Elizabeth play with Lisa while she listens to my recording. Lisa seems calmer and likes going. I get hopeful that this will help her speak better. But Lisa continues to stutter.

And the infections continue. With each new suggestion for a cure, my hopes are raised. After listening to glowing testimonials, we bundle up Lisa and take her to yet another healer. We spend money, confident in this new solution.

But nothing fixes Lisa. Her liver doesn't miraculously begin working normally. Her stutter doesn't go away. It's like I'm on a roller coaster freewheeling from one place to another. After each hopeful high, I come crashing down with the realization that this too is not a permanent fix. I keep looking for a cure.

But there isn't one.

WHAT I LEARNED

Why can't I find a cure? I search and search, willing to try anything. I'm beginning to know as much as the doctors about her medical conditions.

They say I must accept the situation. With each diagnosis, it's an uphill struggle. I don't want to accept anything. I want my daughter to be well.

Acceptance is a hard one. I keep resisting any type of acceptance. But acceptance is the key. Someone told me when we resist something, it persists. But I can't get past myself and my obsession with finding a cure.

As I wrangle with acceptance, I discover a core belief I hold. If I accept Lisa's illness, it means I give up on her, give up on any hope of a future for my daughter.

But that isn't the case at all. Acceptance doesn't mean giving up. I had the two dynamics mixed up.

HOW IT HELPS

What I discover is that acceptance means letting go of an outcome.

When I stop fighting acceptance, life becomes less of a struggle because I'm not expending time and energy running away from acceptance.

In a way, forgiveness is like acceptance. I first thought if I forgive those who have harmed me in the past, I'm condoning their actions. However, my forgiveness releases me from holding on to the hurt I feel. I can let go.

Acceptance is similar to this. By accepting what is happening with Lisa, I'm not giving up, but letting go of my "perceived control" and handing it all over to God, the universe, or whatever there is to believe in.

PRAYER

WHEN THINGS ARE OUT OF CONTROL

"Mommy!" Lisa screams.

I bolt upright in bed. She's sobbing.

"What's the matter, honey?" I sit bedside and pick her up by her shoulders.

"It was a w-w-w-w-w-w-w-olf with r-r-r-r-r-red eyes," she sobs. "It's s-s-s-s-s-s-s-staring at me from the edge of the y-y-y-y-y-y-ard," she struggles out.

It's not the first time she's had this type of nightmare. It's been happening more and more frequently. Her little body shudders. It takes me an hour to calm her down and get her to go back to sleep.

The dream is always the same. She's terrorized by some ominous animal, usually a wolf waiting to get her. A couple nights ago, she dreamt the wolf had caught our golden retriever and was eating it. Last night, she dreamt the wolf was waiting to catch Mark.

WHAT I LEARNED

I call Reverend Jason and ask for help.

He says, "It sounds like Lisa has picked up some negative energy."

I take a deep breath.

"Nothing is stronger than love. No matter how negative the energy, love is stronger," he reiterates. "Call Frances at the Center tomorrow, but for tonight this is what I want you to do."

I take out a pen.

"Do you believe in Jesus?" he asks.

I put the pen down. "Yes, I believe Jesus is a healer

like Buddha and others. That he's a powerful being."

"Good," Jason says. "Jesus is going to help Lisa and you. Light some candles and have them burning throughout the house. Then write these words down because you need to say them like a chant over and over again. Chant them until it feels right to stop."

I pick up the pen again.

He dictates, "In the name and power of Jesus Christ, I command any energy that does not represent love and light to leave now! Right now in the name and power of Jesus Christ, I command any energy that is not of the highest good to leave now."

"I've written it down."

"It's important to say it with emotion and with the knowledge that nothing is stronger than love because that's the ultimate truth. Nothing is stronger than love."

"Are you suggesting Lisa is possessed?" I ask.

"Possession is a hyped-up word, but what it means is that a negative entity may be hanging around Lisa and it doesn't belong there," he says. "There's nothing to be afraid of, for it's fear that a negative entity feeds on."

Oh my, is this even possible?

I do what he suggested. I hold the paper in my hand and with a lit candle in my other hand, I stand in Lisa's room. I read, "In the name and power of Jesus Christ, I command any energy that does not represent love and light to leave now!"

Just the thought of energy playing havoc with my daughter pisses me off.

I say it again with more fierceness. "In the name and power of Jesus Christ, I command any energy that does not represent love and light to leave here now!"

I feel stronger and safer saying these words. Lisa and Michelle are watching me quietly. Lisa seems calmer.

"In the name and power of Jesus Christ, of love, I command any energy that does not represent love and light to leave here now!"

I walk through the house feeling once more in command of the situation. I leave the candles burning for a while as the words repeat in my head.

Lisa fell asleep and didn't wake with a nightmare.

Lisa and I are in a healing circle with Mark. After explaining to Frances the nightmares, we look at her with hope.

A peaceful smile lights up Frances' face. She sits in silence for a few moments. "I'm talking with an entity that seems to feel he has a right to be in Lisa's energy. He's an older gentleman who's very stubborn and doesn't want to know that he's dead." Frances' eyes are closed. She whispers, "I'm explaining to him it's important for him to go toward the light. He doesn't belong here."

We sit in silence. I imagine her speaking to this old man inhabiting my daughter.

"Often times, souls are confused after death, don't know they're dead and don't want to change anything in their lives. So they continue where they've been and cause havoc in the living." She chuckles. "Sometimes it takes a guide to show them the way." She points up toward the window near the ceiling. "Once he understood what happened to him, he was able to see the light and went on his way." She glances up at the window again.

"Was this an exorcism?" I ask, not knowing what

other word to put on it.

"In a sense it is, but it's a word that has too much energy attached to it." She plays with Lisa's fingers.

As usual, Lisa is sleeping in my arms. She's so much bigger now; only her head and torso are in my lap.

"If this was an exorcism, it was so peaceful and full of love. It's nothing like I expected."

"An exorcism guides a wayward soul out of this dimension into the next. That's all it is," Frances says. "It's when there's so much fear that the energy gets out of hand. But there's no need for that." She pats my leg and gets up off the floor.

I stand up.

"I don't think Lisa will have any more problems with nightmares." She turns and guides me out of the chapel. "Let me know how she's doing in a month or two."

HOW IT HELPS

I was amazed how the energy of the words that Jason gave me changed with each recitation. At first, they didn't mean anything but then they brought peace. By the end, I felt empowered.

When I pray, I feel better. It's a way of quieting all the chaos that pulls on me: Lisa's struggles, Michelle's growing pains, and the agony of my marriage. When I'm at church, saying a prayer gives me hope. I believe God is hearing me; or at least, I am hearing me.

Frances was right. Lisa's nightmares are a thing of the past. No more nightmares; no more dreadful visions.

We all get sleep.

MARRIAGE COUNSELING

WHEN THINGS ARE OUT OF CONTROL

It's 1986. We've lived with Lisa's chronic illness for five years. Lisa is starting kindergarten where she will be covered under an Individual Educational Plan (IEP) for special services. Every child in public school who receives special educational services has one. Just in case, I bring along Peggy, an educational advocate, to the meeting with the team of teachers, therapists and the school administrator. As I feared, the administrator says Lisa doesn't need speech therapy. Peggy talks him down.

Lisa loves kindergarten. I feel confused because I want her to have fun and yet it's so hard to leave her anywhere. What if she gets sick?

With both kids in school, I decide to start training to become a court reporter. As a freelance reporter, I will have some modicum of control of my schedule in case Lisa needs me.

Mark is playing racquetball a lot. If he's not working, he's at the racquetball club. Or else out on the river in his boat.

"We don't do anything together anymore," I complain. I glance at the clock. It's 10:10 p.m. He just got home from work.

"You're always busy." He heads towards the fridge.

I grit my teeth. "Do you want a sandwich?"

"No." He changes his mind and heads towards the hallway. "How about learning to play racquetball? I can teach you."

I haven't thought of doing that. I never played any sports in high school. If it's the only way to be together, I'm game. Plus it's another physical activity. "Sure."

My therapist David asks me about my relationship with Mark.

"The racquetball is interesting," I say, glancing at the floor.

"What's going on?" He sees right through me.

"Mark doesn't want to talk about feelings. It's all I want to talk about."

"So the racquetball court is someplace you are at least interacting?"

"Yeah, sometimes we even talk about racquetball."

He squints at me. "Well, it's a start. I've seen relationships heal from the smallest thing."

Lisa has a fever again. We do the usual Dr. Kapher phone call, blood work and chest X-ray. We're off to Boston with a confirmed liver infection. Mark's driving. We don't talk.

We're home from the hospital. Lisa responded quickly to the antibiotics. Now she's on oral antibiotics for two weeks.

I love the folk singer Linda Worster. I heard her sing at the Center of the Light in the Berkshires years ago and I play her music over and over again. She sings a song about watching your loved one sleep and breathing with them. I have this fantasy of listening to this song with Mark.

I play the tape for him after work. He doesn't sit for it, wants to watch TV. I tell him it means something to me. He goes into the kitchen, finds the last piece of chocolate cake, and reads the paper.

I feel very far away from Mark. It's like we're living two different lives. He's on his boat a lot, I'm with the kids. We hardly see each other at racquetball anymore. I feel my world is unraveling. I have so much fear with Lisa off at school and her relentless problems. I crawl into bed at night and cry. Mark just turns away and goes to sleep. I don't understand what is happening.

Mark acts patient but I wonder if he's sick of my sadness. We haven't made love in months. Since I had my tubes tied, birth control is not the issue. I'm like a rubber band always bouncing back to my worrying and sadness. Talking together helps me see his way of coping. It's different than mine. And yet, daily, he gets to walk away from the situation. I cannot get away from it—ever. Even with my court reporting classes, I'm home by the time the kids get home.

WHAT I LEARNED

At the end of 1987, Mark and I decide to go to marriage counseling.

Sharon asks us our goals. My goal is to be happier in my marriage and feel safe. Mark's goal is to be happier as well.

Our counseling sessions seem forced. Sharon encourages us to talk about our emotions. But Mark is trying not to hurt my feelings and I'm holding back because of all of mine.

It's like a catch-22. We've been meeting with the counselor for almost three months. It feels like we're going nowhere.

"You're both so unhappy with each other." Sharon says, looking at each of us. "Have you considered that the steps we may be exploring are to facilitate a parting of ways?"

I'm stunned. I don't want to break up. That was never in my mind. Mark has never had another relationship except with me. I've never wanted to be with anyone else except him. I'm used to his presence; he's a good father. He loves the girls. I love him. I just don't love what's happening between the two of us. I believed that the counseling would clarify what each of us wanted, what was hurting each of us. That it would all be brought into the open and figured out.

I didn't think it would break us up.

Today he says he doesn't want to continue with the counseling sessions. He prefers a trial separation to trying to figure this out. He says he doesn't feel he can be my emotional band-aid anymore. I am devastated. My fists are clenched and my jaw is set. I'm committed to this marriage. I thought he was too.

Mark is moving out. I hear him doing last minute packing. I'm sitting at my steno machine doing my speed building exercises but I'm focusing on each little noise—his footsteps, the creak in the upper dresser drawer. Then I hear him walk through the hallway and out the door. That's it.

I'm sitting here at the machine. My fingers have stopped moving. We're calling it a trial separation. It's easier to live in denial.

But my marriage is over. I'm glad I have work to focus on. Otherwise, I would go crazy.

HOW IT HELPS

Today is my graduation from court reporting school and I'm getting an award. My mother attends my graduation; so does Mark and the girls.

It's a strange feeling, seeing them all in the audience watching me walk down the aisle and receive this award. Who are they seeing? I'm transforming myself in so many ways—the most obvious manifestation of my changes is that I've learned a new skill to support myself. And I'm totally off the meds I started when Lisa was diagnosed.

Of course, the real question is who am I? I have no idea what this new life will be like. I'm in this world and still have trouble making choices for what I want to do. I've re-educated myself so I can support myself. Now what? I work on awareness to be mindful of my thoughts and catch the negative monkey mind. Negative thoughts keep me in negative energy, in the 'loop of poop'. Positive thoughts attract positive energy.

I stare at Mark sitting next to Lisa. Sharon said communication is the key to relationships. Did I fail at Communication 101 because my marriage failed? Having a child with a serious chronic illness puts a tremendous amount of stress on a family unit. Inevitably, each parent reacts differently. In my case, as in many other families, my husband felt the pressure of maintaining the income and the health insurance, thereby preserving the foundational stability of the family. I was the main emotional and physical support for Lisa and Michelle.

Our focuses were different. I felt that he just didn't understand the amount of stress and distress I was in. He seemed to think I was overreacting to her diagnosis and causing the kids to be stressed as well.

But we had differences even before Lisa was born; Lisa's diagnosis brought out those differences. Counseling uncovered the real feelings we didn't want to face. Getting divorced is not easy. But we weren't happy. I could have pretended I was. Lisa's diagnosis helped us weed out the deadwood and uncover who we really are and what we each want.

I try to catch Michelle's eye but she is talking to her dad. Emotions are always changing, moving through us, sometimes just as quickly as our breath moves in and out of our lungs. When they aren't addressed, we spend a great amount of time and energy suppressing our feelings. Mark and I were living in a habitual way and got stuck in that dynamic. He and I had met in high school. We really didn't know what we wanted.

Now, as painful as it is, we both have an opportunity to learn.

I finally catch Michelle's eye and wave. She pokes Lisa and they both wave back, smile, and give me a thumbs up.

ANGER AS A FUEL

WHEN THINGS ARE OUT OF CONTROL

Lisa is a bear this morning. When I take her temperature, it's 101.9. I decide to wait 24 hours before I call the doctor to see if the temperature rectifies itself.

Dr. Kapher finishes the blood work and sends it stat and orders a chest X-ray. We wait for the test results.

Lisa has a liver infection. Once again. We check in to the hospital.

Once again. I could scream. Our lives are an endless routine of 'once agains'.

No one knows how tired I am. No one. I have two stressful jobs: being Lisa's primary caregiver and being a court reporter.

Yet, I am driven from inside. I'll do anything to save her life. I would give up my liver to save her, even though I would die. At least I would be doing something.

I cry and cry. I'm depressed and hopeless and helpless. Where does it get me? Am I really escaping? What will I change for her?

Nothing, she still has the same problem. I have to face it. I have to accept. Lisa has a diseased body. She came into this world like this. Did I do it to her?

I'm angry about so many things. Angry at people saying things they don't mean. Angry at the doctors for using my daughter as a teaching tool as if she's a plastic dummy or punching bag. I'm angry she has a chronic illness that by definition will never go away. I will forever and ever be staring into her pained eyes not able to do anything but cry with her. I'm incredibly angry that something foreign has taken up residence deep inside her, this thing that snuck into her like a pet playing hide and seek. Only, it's not a cute cuddly puppy but a potentially deadly object that she will have to deal with all her life.

I want to pound my fists. I'm so angry I want to kick wildly at something until it hurts. I feel alone and trust no one.

Most of all, I'm angry my life will never be normal again. Not tomorrow, not the next day, not ever. I can't keep living like this.

WHAT I LEARNED

My heart is broken and yet still hopeful. Where does the hope come from? I'm drawn to it like a magnet.

I want to use the energy of my anger to help me speak up, figure out what I need and get it. What's right for me?

I remember once I was visiting my friend Kay. I was upset about something but didn't recognize my own anger.

She smiled. "Oh, you have your angry pants on today, huh?"

What an image, I thought. Angry pants. "Yeah, as a matter of fact, they fit very well," I said with a proud smile on my face. "And they even have suspenders." I owned my anger.

I have a right to feel my anger. I have a right to have anger. I have rights! I also have choices. The choice is mine whether I tune into my monkey mind or my higher self. Do I try to control or do I trust? Do I ignore everything good in my life or do I appreciate what I have? Do I choose to be blocked—to sit and cry—or do I find something creative to do, even if it's something simple like coloring?

I decide to check in with myself. Feeling that seething inside, I sit down and write out word for word what I'm angry about. When I can't think of another thing, I stare at the words "I AM ANGRY AT." It triggers more feelings of anger and I write those.

HOW IT HELPS

Anger sneaks up on us with the delivery of devastating news that changes the course of our lives. What does one do with that anger? It's important to feel the anger, and what we do with it is equally important. Anger is fuel we can turn on ourselves and hurt ourselves or others.

Or, we can use anger to take action towards a positive goal. Think about the power of anger. It's an engine that needs direction, like the engine in one's car. It's running; which way will the wheels take me? I can use the anger in a proactive way to take action in order to make a positive change. If nothing else, the action itself helps ease the helplessness.

When I started the support group, I began funneling my anger toward a positive goal. It was a positive action that relieved some of my helplessness.

By checking in with myself and writing out my anger, I feel the power of that anger. By expressing it, I can then make a list of actions to take.

And all the while, I'm wearing my angry pants.

CHRONIC SORROW

WHEN THINGS ARE OUT OF CONTROL

Lisa is seven years old today. I'm noticing how she gets aggravated with Michelle and she starts a fight. She'll start screaming and slam the door or break one of her toys. Once, she broke a window.

She seems angry at the world. I'm at a loss how to deal with it. At first, it was doctors and hospitals and the struggle to keep her alive. Then it became therapists dealing with her developmental problems. Now we have to cope with her emotional trauma.

I'm remembering that day long ago when the words chronic illness finally filtered into my own traumatized brain. Up to that moment, I had been living in the belief that there would be a quick fix and we'd get back to normal.

I never once imagined the depth of struggle that chronic illness brings. It never stops. Now it's her anger. I read somewhere that the liver represents anger.

The usual signs appear again. Fever and crabbiness. We go through the usual motions with Dr. Kapher. I fall into a tailspin. For a brief moment, I had been thinking we were beyond that and onto the other aspects of chronic illness.

But no, chronic is chronic. Lisa has a liver infection again. We head to Boston Children's Hospital.

There is no fix. This trip will not fix her. I'll be in this hell the rest of my life.

WHAT I LEARNED

I'm sitting in Lisa's hospital room. She'll be here for a week. I journal. Sometimes I wonder what's the point.

What have I learned? To stay in the present or at least try to. To ask for help. I get to choose what I share and who I share it with. I know what a panic attack is and know the signs and have tools to stop it.

But there has to be more, something that captures what I'm going through.

I'm in the library at the University of Massachusetts. It's tall, higher than most, if not all, the buildings on campus. When they first built it, the windows would pop out in the wind. I've decided to start researching living with the chronic illness of a child. I'm poring through microfiche cards from *Psychology Today* and other journals.

Words flash by my eyes. And then, there on the screen, I see two words.

Chronic sorrow.

It's the recurring intense feelings of grief in the lives of parents dealing with children with chronic illness.

As I continue reading, I feel the tears well up behind my eyes. They use the words "normal" and "living loss", the difference between "what is" and "what should have been." I feel the deep chasm in my heart and now know that there's a term for what I'm experiencing as a parent, as a caregiver, as a person. Lisa has a chronic illness and I have chronic sorrow.

HOW IT HELPS

Finding the article on chronic sorrow brings me such clarity. It feels like the missing puzzle piece in my daily roller coaster of emotions. Chronic illness is a cycle: the illness does not go away, the problems do not go away, nothing gets fixed, it just keeps repeating itself. With every new diagnosis, the full force of the illness comes back at me and I'm grieving again. As a result, the living loss is ongoing, chronic, and painful.

Having tools helps me cope with my life. By educating myself, I'm armed to deal with the challenges that arise.

CREATIVE OUTLETS

WHEN THINGS ARE OUT OF CONTROL

It's the first day of school. I cry when Michelle boards the bus. Lisa gets picked up by a special education van.

I have four hours of free time. Just for myself. I walk around the house a little uncertain what to do. I mean, there was a time before I was married where I was just me. It feels so long ago I can't remember it. We gather people around us we call a family and we become one with it.

But at this moment, I'm all alone. It's just me. What will I do with myself? Unable to think of anything else, I catch up on some work.

Mark takes the girls out to celebrate Michelle's ninth birthday. When he returns, we go for a walk. He admits he is scared of all the changes. I tell him I'm scared too. I want to hit him really hard, kick him. I'm so angry. I smack him on the arm as we walk.

He doesn't want to come home.

WHAT I LEARNED

I realize I need a hobby, something to physically do with my hands, something that doesn't take a lot of brain power, but is repetitive and keeps me busy.

I decide to try knitting or crocheting. I like the latter better and start crocheting a quilt square by square. It helps me pass the time at Boston Children's and has a calming effect. When I find it a challenge to be in public, I find doing something in a quiet setting comforting.

I also start walking with a friend because it's also beneficial. And reading on an exercise bike keeps my mind busy and my body moving. Sometimes, I just sit in my rocking chair. I find the movement comforting.

HOW IT HELPS

Physical exercise has a positive effect on the body, mind and our emotions. It releases endorphins. When my friend and I walk down the back roads past houses and trees, we talk. Every part of it is an outlet.

I also learn about educational kinesiology which is a way to learn through movement. The premise is that bilateral and contralateral movements improve the body-mind connection. Brain Gym exercises embody this principle in a very calming way.

I go to a choir rehearsal and we try a song but it doesn't sound so great. The director stops us and runs us through some of these Brain Gym exercises. I love the cross crawl which engages both sides of our brains. After the exercise, we start singing. We blend so much better. I can hear the other singers, they can hear me. During one of the songs, we have some choreographed movements. We move like we're one person.

I find music and being inspired by beauty raises my energy and makes me feel better.

I remember once I was alone in the car feeling bereft. I turned the radio on and heard a song I knew. I didn't feel like singing along but I made myself say the words and then I started singing. It was a three-minute reprieve. When it was over, my mood had lifted. That's the power of song.

SELF-HELP BOOKS

WHEN THINGS ARE OUT OF CONTROL

I'm a divorced parent, weighed down by my work and need of money. That isn't all there is of me, right? But I only believe in myself if others believe in me. My therapist says that's a problem. I need to be strong for myself and not rely on someone else.

It all just feels too much. Tears are falling down my face. My mouth is contorted and I feel small. Am I a little girl stuck in a grown woman's world of problems? Do I dare do something different and wander outside my sense of safety?

Today is Sunday. We usually visit my mom on a Friday or Saturday. What if I visited tonight? Would I be okay? Can I handle the decision? It's really all up to me.

I'm lonely for a cheerleader, someone who stands at my side and says, "You can do it. You're good enough. You're innocent." Where's my inside cheerleader? Where am I when it comes to believing in myself? I'm mute. I'm small and I'm mute. Why can't I believe in myself? I'm crying inside and out. Who's going to save me? Who's going to bail me out when I'm wrong? Who's going to put me back together when I've fallen apart? Who?

My choices have dwindled down to one person— me. No one else can do it. If anyone comes along and tells me I'm good, I'm innocent, I'm okay, it's just going to be a false sense that I hold onto because the truth is it needs to come from me. ME. Isn't that the point? I need to rely on me. ME, I scream. Won't you answer me???

I feel like I'm up against the fear I've been running from for so long. My fear of failure, my fear that everyone really will find out what I'm all about: I can't do it and I can't figure out how.

But listen to all my negative words. Listen to what I'm feeding myself. Where did this come from and who else is inside me that can help?

I've gotten through a lot of stuff. I've fought illness. I've helped myself many times. I remember staring at snot on the floor as I once lay there crying so many years ago giving up on everything. Well, here I am again, only this time it's a slow, painful dissolving of the 'me' I thought I was, because the new ME is emerging. Can't anyone hear me screaming? I'm melting like the Wicked Witch of the West and it's not pretty. I'm scared.

There's such chaos around me. It's hard to think when the one I'm trying to figure out is crying inside. It is my inner little girl who is so sad and alone.

Where is my adult self?

WHAT I LEARNED

I find a book called *Feel the Fear and Do It Anyway* by Susan Jeffers. I like the title. It sounds like something I need to read. All my life I've lived in fear. My therapists have pointed this out to me and now I see it. I remember what my therapist said, I can wallow around in why I'm like this or else I can get on with my life. That's why I was attracted to this book. I'm feeling the fear, but how do I keep going?

The book says that, as long as I continue to grow, fear will never go away. It's a daunting thought. I want to be relieved of my fear but this is saying I will always have it. I've faced all those doctors. I didn't want to but I did it. Now I'm out there facing my fear of failing as a court reporter and of raising two children alone. I'm facing my fears.

I read more of the book. It says the only way to feel better about myself is to go out and do whatever I have to do. Not only am I going to experience fear doing something new, but so is everyone else.

I guess I don't think of other people's fear. I get so caught up in my own that I forget others feel the same way. Somehow, they do new things while I get stuck in immobilizing terror. And yet, my life is changing and I am surviving.

The author Susan Jeffers says that pushing through my fear is less frightening than living with the underlying fear that comes from a feeling of helplessness. I have to think on that one.

I worry about making decisions. I worry about being wrong. I worry about my safety. I worry about life in general. I worry about Lisa and her infections. I worry about everything. The book gives techniques for turning fear, indecision and anger into power and positive action. I find an affirmation I like: "Whatever happens to me, given any situation, I can handle it!"

I keep repeating it. It's my new goal.

HOW IT HELPS

Reading Jeffers' books feels like someone writing about me. I'm amazed by the similarities. Finding a book that I resonate with really helps me feel supported. I love to go into the self-help section in a bookstore and just read titles and feel my reaction to the titles. More often than not, my interest is piqued when the book has a message for me. I do not feel so alone.

I'm thinking a lot about feeling my fear. I've learned 90% of what I worry about never comes true. I can choose to hold my fear in a place of pain or from a place of power. When I come from a place of power, I look at my responsibility for a situation. I want to notice if I blame anyone else for anything I am being, doing or feeling. Usually my style is to judge and blame myself, pound me down with what I think other people are feeling about me. It's an old habit I developed from my father who always judged us harshly. I figure if I put myself down, it won't hurt so much when someone else judges me.

I also grew up believing crying is shameful. My father would yell at me not to cry.

I'm sitting in my therapist's office. He says, "Crying is a necessary expression of emotion."

"It is? I felt such judgment when I cried in my house."

"It releases emotions to make room for more. It's like a baptism of tears. Like they're blessing you."

I like that image. Deep down, it feels true. I can think more clearly and be more present once I've cried.

MEDITATION

WHEN THINGS ARE OUT OF CONTROL

My divorce became final today. It's so odd that we reached this situation. This divorce is not what I want. We were supposed to be together for the rest of our lives. Instead, Mark and I are done.

Michelle and Lisa start school, fifth and third grades. I find myself struggling every day. I'm so afraid of Lisa getting sick. I'm confused about where to put my efforts in my life. My work demands my attention. I want more parental support. I don't know if it's fear that stops me from acting on things or am I just tired?

It's 4:00 a.m. I can't sleep and I'm feeling anxious. It's been a very hard lesson to learn to accept that I have no power over Lisa's disease. Even though I accept what is happening, I still spend time learning all I can about her illness. I have to. I know it's wrong, but I still have the belief that if I learn it all, I can tell the doctors what to do and they will fix it. But I cannot.

I can't cure her and I hate it!

WHAT I LEARNED

I realize meditation might help me sleep at night. I don't know enough about it and find a class that will last for eight weeks. The stated goal is to cultivate a deeper relationship with ourselves as we develop meditative tools.

Soft music plays in the background. "The wisp of smoke rises up in the air like a spiral," Ellen says in her soft voice. "My breath flows in and out as I focus on the spiraling energy. Follow the spiral up and up. If you get distracted, let the music help you follow the spiral."

This exercise raises energy. With my eyes closed, I can see the big empty space. Wide open nothingness and yet it feels like a pool of warm water where I float in comfort in the vastness. I feel wonderful.

HOW IT HELPS

Using the energy-raising techniques I learned in the meditation class, I'm able to connect into a higher place. My head feels slightly light and a pressure develops in the back of my neck almost like energy is filling up there. This light tingle tells me I'm raising my energy. I become a larger presence in the room and take up more space energetically. It is comforting.

Sitting with myself in meditation gives me a feeling of calmness most of the time. I know I have a monkey mind that flits from worry to worry. There are many times I try to stop my mind from distracting thoughts but can't. But I don't have to be a slave to my obsessive thoughts. I can stop struggling and change my mood by playing a CD of sitar music, chant, use prayer beads, light incense, or even do a walking meditation.

This method of focusing my mind extends to activities in general. When the monkey mind starts, no matter what I am doing, if I can, I move on to another activity. The goal is to let go without judgment and move on.

I've practiced meditation and connected with my higher self. At times, I feel deeply connected with the universal wisdom, my higher wisdom and other entities of light. I feel great comfort and support from these experiences. I've no explanation other than these experiences have helped me feel better. I have no need to prove whether they're true or not. These experiences are true for me.

It's 2:00 a.m. and I can't sleep. I put on a meditation CD.

"Begin by making yourself comfortable. Now take three long, slow deep breaths. Take your time and enjoy the luxury of these breaths. Be aware of your body and let it relax more with each breath. If you feel tension in parts of your body, let your awareness relax into these areas.

"Begin now to focus on your heart and solar plexus. Imagine a warm light radiating out like a healing sun. Its relaxing rays are filling every area of your body…"

I fall asleep.

# POSITIVE AFFIRMATIONS

WHEN THINGS ARE OUT OF CONTROL

It's three days after Lisa's ninth birthday and we're in the car on the way to Boston Children's Hospital. We did the customary blood work, X-ray and call to Dr. Gold. I have to talk to Dr. Gold about bypassing the X-ray. It's obvious when she gets sick, it's her liver. I want to end the needless exposure to more radiation every time she's ill.

Lisa is being discharged today on oral antibiotics. The doctors feel the three-month stint on antibiotics is not long enough. They're extending it to six months. They have concerns about her becoming immune to the antibiotics, but feel this step is conservative enough to warrant the six months.

I worry about what's going to happen. I'm feeling the burden of chronic sorrow pounding at my heart. I took the assertiveness training but I'm not using anything I learned. Everything feels too much. I'm not reaching for anything else I've learned because I can't get away from myself or my worries about Lisa.

I have to do something. I can't keep on living like this. I will collapse under this fear.

WHAT I LEARNED

Worry is the fuel for the chatterbox. Worry about the future. Worry about what's happened in the past. Worry for what is not known. In my opinion, worry feeds an illness and makes it worse. I understand it reduces blood flow which restricts healing. Worry stifles

97

life, diminishes light and love and encourages depression and lower energy.

Worry creates distractions that take me away from my centeredness and balance. Worry is a negative tool that undermines my well-being. It takes mindfulness to interrupt my thoughts, redirecting and reframing scenarios in my head. Like a slap in the face, refocusing my mind helps disarm the loop of worry I get stuck in.

Someone suggested affirmations as a powerful way to silence the chatterbox. Our internal voice of doom and gloom will probably never go away so naming it allows me to befriend my chatterbox and communicate with it: a short, concise sentence identifying the essence I want.

I could create an affirmation LISA IS HEALTHY or MARK LOVES ME, but I don't have control over Lisa or Mark. I have control over me.

When the chatterbox starts up, I acknowledge it's there and then tune into a higher way of thinking. It's never really going to go away but I can redirect it.

HOW IT HELPS

I try it. I write out four affirmations on index cards.

I AM SAFE
I MAKE DECISIONS EASILY
I AM SURROUNDED BY POSITIVE PEOPLE
I LOVE MYSELF

I stare at them and repeat the words out loud and then place the cards in strategic locations: on the mirrors in the bathroom and bedroom, in my car, on the refrigerator.

Over the weeks, I look at them so often I stop noticing the cards. But I realize they're giving me subliminal messages. I can feel my attitude and my demeanor becoming more positive.

Sometimes the phrase doesn't do anything for me. I changed two of the affirmations and replaced them with more powerful words, eliciting the feeling I want.

I AM SURROUNDED BY LOVING PEOPLE
I AM CONFIDENT

The rule of thumb with affirmations is to state them in the positive after the words "I am." Stay away from words you don't want to enforce such as "I am not anxious" as that phrase is accentuating the word "anxious." Louise Hay has written several books on positive affirmations, and she has CDs available as well.

Another technique I use when I am feeling negative about myself is to list 10 positive things about me. Not just think them but write them down.

Here goes: I am honest. I am loving. I love nature. I love animals. I love to sing. I love mountaintops. I am a good mother. I love to drive a car. I am a good speller. I am courageous.

My best guess why this works is that this list rewrites the pathways in my mind away from my negative thoughts. After all, for how many years as a child was I programmed by the negative comments of my father? I'm reprogramming those pathways.

I feel better because I said my list. I know Lisa will get sick again but I'm not worrying at the moment. We just celebrated her ninth birthday. The doctors said she wouldn't live past the age of two and look at her now.

Lisa told me she's naming her liver. "Olga. I'm going to call it Olga."

"Olga sounds stubborn."

She says, "Exactly."

SETTING BOUNDARIES

WHEN THINGS ARE OUT OF CONTROL

My father has been judgmental for as long as I can remember. He'd swear and call us names, blame me for mess ups he made. Early on, I learned to think like him so that I wouldn't be surprised by any of his thoughts and actions. I learned to always be aware of everyone's emotional state so that I could protect myself. And to judge myself with little or no mercy.

Once a month, on a Friday or Saturday, I take the girls down to my parents' house for dinner.

We're sitting in the driveway in the car. I turn to the girls. "We're going to have a visit. If we have to leave quickly, I don't want any arguments. Understood?"

They nod their heads.

"I mean it."

My mother always has something to show me—an article from the newspaper or something else she read. Today, it's an article about one of her ancestors.

My father doesn't interact with the girls or even hug them. If something isn't part of his routine, he isn't happy. We move around him with carefulness, on guard.

Dinner is always excruciating. "Are you working?" he barks out.

"Yes." I never say more than a one-word answer.

He sneers as he finishes his roast pork. "You're getting fat."

I stare ahead, gritting my teeth.

As soon as I can get away from the table, I go into the den. The girls are playing with the few toys my mother keeps in the house.

"We've gotta go." They ignore me. I say it louder, "We've gotta go. Now!"

They scramble up and follow me out the door.

It's past midnight and Lisa is having a tantrum—screaming, crying, and slamming the door. It started about 10:15. She tried to make a Valentine's card and then she felt that it didn't look as good as everyone else's.

Her outburst catapults me back to the halls of the hospital with her crying and wailing. I'm triggered and do whatever I can to keep breathing. Her tears always bring out this helpless energy that feels horrible. She has too much power.

I'm very tired. This night was exhausting. It's a reminder of why I don't like to do things with her and why I have no patience. And her emotional outbursts seem to be happening more often.

I feel I'm knee deep in a sinking ship. Water is coming in fast. Do I stay on this ship? What choice do I have?

WHAT I LEARNED

I need to deal with Lisa's temper tantrums. We make an appointment with Dr. Peter Steinman, a child psychologist/counselor. He's known for working with children in challenging situations.

I tell Peter about her meltdowns—how she hits, breaks windows, slams doors, and breaks toys.

"She pushes me around, literally. She's getting as tall as me."

He explains that Lisa is terrified of the world and what it has to offer her. "You are her safe person. She needs someone strong enough to kick against so she feels safer. She needs you to be strong."

I stare at him. I think about strong walls that sometimes take my own kicks. It makes sense. I need to be strong. "Let her literally kick me?"

Gently, Peter says, "You have to set limits on what is acceptable within her tantrums and expressions of fear and anger."

I'm not used to thinking about boundaries. I need to, though, so she has room to express her feelings but not hurt me. "I don't know how."

"You came to the right place."

We do some role playing about boundaries. He points out to the girls how much better it feels to be heard, without fighting and without interruptions.

And then he takes us into his playroom next to his office. It's filled with soft pillows and airguns that pop balls. "Go at it. See who can hit the other the most."

We stare at him and then burst out laughing. I think I took the most pillow hits but I got my fair share in as well.

Afterwards, we're joking with each other back in his office.

"C-c-c-c-c-an we do this ag-g-g-g-g-g-g-g-ain?" Lisa asks.

"Sure," Peter smiles. "And let's recap ways to express it if we aren't feeling heard."

As we leave, he hands me a sheet of paper listing boundaries.

I also decide to meet privately with Helena, a healer. She tells me that my inner little girl is curled up tight in a terrified ball and immobilized by fear. As she tells me this, I feel it.

I get a flavor of the tyrant my father is, that his will is very strong—and his level of fear so high that he has built a thick fortress around his feelings and remains in control to stay safe. Helena helps me understand how his life has played out with this fear level, and how much pain he's in.

We talk about his level of control and what he could possibly learn in this life.

Helena says, "Go ahead. Speak to his higher self."

I stiffen in my chair but her smile reminds me I'm safe. I begin, "It's not my responsibility to educate you, Dad." I shut my eyes and continue. "The pain you feel and your control over yourself is no longer going to control me." I take a deep breath. "It's no longer going to control this very hurt girl inside me. I'm a good person and all I want to do is to love you and be loved." I'm crying but I feel my energy shift. I'm feeling more compassion towards him.

But, still, I'm terrified of him. To protect myself, Helena suggests I treat him like a neighbor and be cordial as I begin to build my fortress to protect my terrified inner child.

HOW IT HELPS

Experiencing my voice and speaking up for myself helps me feel stronger. I never learned personal boundaries as a child. I had no role model. Through therapy, I learned I have personal space that is mine alone. I have physical and emotional boundaries.

Boundaries give us a sense of safety in this crazy world. We can learn to define our personal boundaries and upon recognizing these boundaries, we can speak up and take care of ourselves.

Every time I learn a technique to make myself a stronger person, I share this gift with both of my girls.

FACILITATED SUPPORT GROUPS

WHEN THINGS ARE OUT OF CONTROL

Lisa is 11 years old and her last ultrasound showed the blood flow in her liver is going forward whereas, last year, it was going backwards. She wasn't supposed to live past the age of two without a transplant. Now, she's doing great.

We go on a camping vacation. One afternoon, Lisa gets it into her head that she wants an ice cream cone.

"No," I say, "it's too close to dinner."

She keeps asking and I keep saying no. She presses the issue. We are at our campsite with other families around us able to hear everything. It takes all my power not to give in.

She has a complete meltdown. I'm feeling humiliated by my child having a tantrum. Lisa's voice goes hoarse as she begs and pleads. She flails out and tries to hit me. I ask myself whether this is really over an ice cream cone or does it have everything to do with her illness, hospitalizations, pain, and infections. And her fear of the future. I'm triggered by her anger. She screams she hates me and never wants to talk to me ever again.

She starts to shake while she cries. Finally, she stands pathetically by the tent, like she's defeated. It takes everything out of her. Out of me as well. But I'm the adult and I have to make dinner.

After a week away on vacation, we come home to a message on our answering machine. "This is Dr.

Argiles. Dr. Gold is recommending Lisa be put on a liver transplant list. Call me when you get this message so we can make the necessary plans for her admission to the hospital."

"What!!" I scream. He wants what?? Why a transplant list now? I thought we were beyond that. Is this going to solve everything or are we descending into another level of the Twilight Zone?

What will a transplant mean at 11 years old? I want to feel excitement but I cannot go there.

Lisa is going to be admitted to Tufts New England Medical Center for a week-long workup for placing her on the transplant list. She'll miss school. I'm told a transplant workup is likened to what astronauts go through before they go into space.

It's Lisa's first day of school. I look at each milestone differently now. Will this be the last first day where her new classmates and teacher have to deal with her chronic problems? Will it be her last first day ever? October is still a full month away.

I don't know how I'm getting through each day.

We arrive at Tufts at 9:30 a.m. Lisa is scheduled for a complete medical assessment: laboratory assessment, chest X-ray, ultrasound with Doppler, CT scan, MRI, total body bone scan, hepatic angiogram, cholangiogram, electrocardiogram, echocardiogram, Persantine thallium stress test, pulmonary function tests, upper endoscopy, lower endoscopy, kidney tests, a psychosocial assessment and a nutritional assessment.

We're to be here for a week.

At the end of the week, we leave the hospital. The tests are all done. We have to wait for the results. In

1981, her doctors didn't expect her to live past the age of two. We showed them. At what cost though? A family torn apart, endless trips to doctors and hospitals. My sanity.

A week passes. Dr. Gold calls. Lisa's liver is functioning well enough so that they cannot justify putting her on the transplant list. Even with all the infections, that's not a reason to transplant her liver. Her transplant status is set to 'Inactive' unless her condition changes.

What do we do now?

WHAT I LEARNED

This last hospitalization and transplant list status upends us and brings me back to chronic sorrow. Again, I go through feeling the cycles of sorrow and am left with the reminder that chronic sorrow indeed is part of my life.

I have to do something to help myself. I remember how asking for help is a good tool. I start thinking about the failed support group I began when Lisa was two. Parents really need support; maybe there is another way to run a support group.

My pediatrician recommends Connie, a pediatric social worker I can get help from to create a new group. Connie gives me a list of rules for a safe environment. I advertise in the local paper and tell doctors.

I call the group "Our Care" and we begin meeting twice a month on Friday in the waiting room of a local pediatrician's office.

At the first monthly Friday meeting, I announce a topic. For the second, I bring in a speaker. Connie and I meet once during each month to evaluate the group's process.

I have a sign on display for every meeting.

Ground Rules
Confidentiality - What you hear here, stays here
Share feelings and experiences, but not advice
No cross-talk
Accept each other without making judgments
Avoid interrupting or having side conversations
Be respectful and sensitive to others
Be supporting and encouraging to others

One of our guest speakers is a massage therapist offering tips on self-care. Another speaker is Peggy, the educational advocate who helped me with Lisa's Individual Educational Plan. Other speakers include a creative arts teacher who helps us find our creative processes; a local doctor helping us learn to communicate more clearly with physicians; and many others.

I write a grant proposal to get support. The money pays for snacks, ads, and babysitting costs for single parents.

One night, one of the mothers brings in an essay by Emily Perl Kingsley called *Welcome to Holland*. The mother explains to us that having a child with a disability is like going into a parallel world. "Your expectations are one place, the reality you are thrust into is another place."

We all nod our heads.

The mother continues. "It's as if we expected to be in Italy when we got on the plane but deplaned to find ourselves in Holland. Both are good places, only different from each other."

HOW IT HELPS

After one of the meetings, I dream about mothers. I dream about the challenge moms have in finding their identity beyond their chronically-ill kids and I encourage them to speak up for themselves. In the group, during the introductions, we ask moms to talk mostly about themselves. It's challenging, since moms are so identified with their children. They have forgotten who they were. We help them remember.

I'm letting go of the dream of expecting to be 'in Italy' with a perfect baby. I can celebrate Lisa as the beautiful child she is. I can live 'in Holland' and find the joys it contains.

Having this understanding helps me to carry on. The sharing and the speakers' insights help. I continue putting one foot in front of another, giving myself latitude for my emotional ups and downs, growing from what I learn every day and remaining as calm as I can in the developments. I am a barometer for my children. When I fall apart, they fall apart. It's a heavy burden to carry, but one that I would not want anyone else to bear.

SIBLING REACTIONS

WHEN THINGS ARE OUT OF CONTROL

We settle Lisa on the couch in the living room. "I want to stay with the family, not down in my bedroom," she says as she winces in pain, exhausted from yet another hospitalization. She's 15 years old and takes up the length of the couch. We spent a week at Tufts New England Medical Center while the GI team got Lisa's liver infection under control.

Discharge instructions include a cocktail of three IV antibiotics. The medical supplies arrive and stand waiting in large boxes near the front door. The IV antibiotic medications, IV lines, caps, ends, Heparin and saline-filled syringes, alcohol wipes, an IV pole—the list goes on with all the supplies needed for 21 days of dosage for three different antibiotics. The doctors haven't been able to isolate the bacteria infecting her liver, so their choice comes down to three different broad-based antibiotics—"big guns" as we say.

The visiting nurse arrives to go over the intricate and complicated instructions with timing and dosing of the drugs. One antibiotic is every three hours and the other two every four hours. Change the IV lines every three times so I have to remember to date the lines on the little piece of tape to keep track. There are three separate lines. Her IV site is a sterile access so must be wiped three times with an alcohol swab. Keep the connecting IV line sterile. Then when done, wipe clean again and cap off. Watch for swelling, redness, heat or pain around the IV site. Lisa wants to do her own connecting to the meds when she feels better, but now she's completely dependent on me. I know she's listening intently to the nurse and will follow my steps to make sure I'm doing it right. We're a team.

My concentration is totally on the nurse. I don't notice Michelle come downstairs. "Mom, I don't feel well. I think I'm sick."

At first, I'm not listening.

"I don't feel well," Michelle repeats. Then she sits on the edge of the couch by Lisa's feet and lays across Lisa's legs.

I stare at her, wanting to scream, "Get off of her!" But I don't. I look at the visiting nurse and she looks at me, both wanting to say something but withholding.

WHAT I LEARNED

In our support group, this topic of siblings of children with special needs had come up. They carry unusual concerns for their brother or sister. There are familiar themes such as over-identification, embarrassment, guilt, isolation, loneliness and loss, increased responsibilities, and pressure to achieve.

Michelle is demonstrating she's feeling left out. Maybe she is getting sick, but more likely, she's over-identifying with Lisa's illness and making herself feel ill enough to believe she's getting sick.

HOW IT HELPS

After the nurse leaves, I sit down in the recliner and gesture for Michelle to come sit on my lap. Her long legs hang over the sides. She puts her head on my chest. I hold her for a few moments of silence stroking her hair. I ask her what hurts.

Having learned about sibling reactions helped me find compassion when Michelle splayed her body over

Lisa's and claimed she was ill as well. Finding my compassion helped me gently be outside of my own pain for a while and let me be there for Michelle and for myself.

It's not easy nor simple to do this, but siblings are part of the family in crisis too. This was a wake-up call for me to remember Michelle has needs too.

SELF-MASSAGE

WHEN THINGS ARE OUT OF CONTROL

Lisa turned 18 last week. We go to her doctor's for a checkup. The nurse comes out into the waiting room and stands in front of us. "Lisa, now that you're 18, you have a choice to come in by yourself or you can have your mom join you. It's up to you."

I'm stunned. I'm not going to be in on every word?

"My m-m-m-m-om can j-j-j-j-j-j-oin us."

I am thankful. I know it's healthy to put the decisions in Lisa's hands, but will she survive without me in control?

The doctor says, "Breathe." Lisa takes a full breath and I do too. It's a few seconds before I realize that he's not talking to me. I'm not the patient. I can't breathe for her.

WHAT I LEARNED

Even a simple doctor's visit puts me on edge. There may come a time Lisa chooses to be in the exam room by herself.

She's becoming an adult. Parents and children separate. I separated from my father even before he died five years ago. As for my mother, I would never consider letting her into a doctor's visit with me.

I have to remember to help myself and not just in terms of my mental health. I've been learning to massage my palms and feet. I'm sure there are reflexology reasons to do this; I just know it feels good and relaxes me.

There's a great book called *Energy Medicine* by Donna Eden. She describes energy points on our bodies that can be massaged so that negative energy is released. I like the "Oh My God" points on the forehead: massaging a spot above each eyebrow and holding the temples while thinking of a negative experience is a great way to release the memory. Another one is the Wayne Cook position that she recommends when one is overwhelmed or hysterical. It involves crossing your legs, holding your foot, and breathing. It lets your energy flow smoothly through your body.

There are locations on your body to calm you down by tapping them, such as the K27 points below your clavicle. Thumping your thymus gland right in the center of your chest gives you more energy.

Eden also talks about zipping up your central meridian. This protects you from other people's negative energy.

I came across a technique called EFT (Emotional Freedom Technique) that is a series of tappings on certain parts of the face and hands that can help release stress. There are YouTube videos of war veterans actually demonstrating the technique while talking about their panic attacks and triggers, and one can see in real-time the calming effects of EFT.

Another helpful tool is holding a small smooth stone; someone referred to it as a worry stone. I can fiddle with it, rub my fingers on it, keep it in my pocket and work on it when I feel an increase in my anxiety.

HOW IT HELPS

Lisa is graduating from high school today. As I watch her cross the stage and receive her diploma, my eyes tear up with joy. A month ago, she was hospitalized with a liver infection. After 10 days, she was released with the normal IV antibiotic treatment. I worried whether she was going to be able to make today's graduation. If I had to, I would have wheeled her across the stage. But she's doing it herself. I wipe my eyes.

Acceptance is just a word. How to live in acceptance is a process and a challenge. Understanding chronic sorrow helps with his process.

I feel for my small worry stone in my pocket and smile. It helps me remember I'm an energy body as well as a physical body. Ancient therapies such as acupuncture and acupressure are proven methods of tapping into the energy body. Many modalities can help; I'm finding the ones that work for me.

FORGIVENESS

WHEN THINGS ARE OUT OF CONTROL

I'm sitting in the backyard of Michelle's house holding my six-month-old grandson Jackson. Michelle's been married five years to Eric and they live about 30 minutes away. He's a blessing, this little boy, and his joy in being with me fills my heart.

Lisa is 29 years old. After high school, she went on to study business at college. We found one that accommodated special needs students, helping her with test-taking and speech. Today, she's a bookkeeper helping disabled and chronically-ill people. The company understands chronic illness and adjusts when she's hospitalized for infections which is about once a year now. The Family and Medical Leave Act ensures she doesn't lose her job when she's out for extended periods of time.

I could say everything is fine, but that's not true. In college, Lisa took up smoking. It started from peer pressure but she says it helps calm her down. I hate it.

The other thing is that my mother's health is failing and we've put her in a nursing home. She needs dialysis and her lungs are failing.

WHAT I LEARNED

I visit my mom in the nursing home. She's so frail. As I push her wheelchair out to the sunroom, I'm remembering the way she used to save articles for me to read. She and my father did the best they could. Parenting is hard. We make decisions that children don't understand or agree with. We can't hang on to the resentments of our parents for our whole lives. At some point, we have to let go.

Eckhart Tolle talks about surrendered action, giving into what is around you and what you are doing. Performing an action in the state of acceptance brings you peace.

I forgive my mother. I'm not sure I'm ready to forgive my father, but at least I'm taking this action. I forgive my mother for not being stronger, for not protecting me, for not being there when I needed her help around Lisa's illness.

I have to forgive everyone I can. I forgive the doctors for not being able to fix Lisa. I forgive the surgeons. I forgive the medications.

I even forgive Lisa for being ill. I forgive her for smoking even though I wish she wouldn't. She's doing the best she can.

I write a letter to her.

You are the most courageous person I have ever met. For what you've had to face in your life, you deal with it like a soldier in battle knowing you must win, for it means your freedom of spirit. Instead of taking the easy paths, you choose the higher roads that lead to your self-respect, your self-love. I don't know another person on this Earth that works harder than you. I commend you. I am so proud of you. The wars you have personally fought are won again and again. Sometimes you need to enlist support and you do.

I am also very proud to say you have support. Both your Dad and I are here for you. You rally your call for help and we come. That's because we are a team. We are behind you. We've got your back.

I will never stop answering your call for help. My heart is filled with love for you, a deep love that lasts through lifetimes. Never will you be without my love and support, without my strength to draw upon, and without my deep respect and admiration.

I know your battle. I taste your tears. I feel your will to conquer. Keep fighting always. When you feel discouraged, remember the stones of your foundation are steady and true. Your Mom and Dad, we're always here for you.

HOW IT HELPS

I know my mother will pass out of this life soon. I am grateful I can spend these last few months with her not wanting anything from her. By forgiving her, I'm freeing myself from holding onto any hurt.

"Mom, are you ready to go back to your room?" I adjust the blanket around her legs.

"Just a little more sun. It's so pretty out here."

I smile and sidle up closer to her.

GRATITUDE

WHEN THINGS ARE OUT OF CONTROL

I'm looking at family pictures. Lisa is 30 years old. I'm feeling intensely sad. Maybe it's from the pictures, gazing into the eyes of so long ago relatives and friends. Maybe it's visiting my mom in the nursing home, talking about her wishes and holding hope for her. Maybe it's thinking ahead to Saturday when I accompany Lisa to her pain management appointment supporting her as she undergoes a procedure to stop the unrelenting pain in her liver. Or maybe it's a global sadness over our abuse of this Earth and the garbage, litter and lack of recycling.

I guess my sadness lies in everything above. So where is my hope? Where is my excitement for my grandson as he eagerly walks his freedom at 14 months? And the new life growing in Michelle's womb. A little girl we don't know yet, who is gathering speed in every cell.

WHAT I LEARNED

I do something outrageous. I go on a firewalk.

A group of about 40 people, both men and women, gather at about 2:00 p.m. in a field. Our first task is to build the fire. We each place logs in a large pyramid and then light it. The bonfire burns into the late afternoon and evening. The group of us stands holding hands around the fire listening to the instructor. We sing songs, chant, and bond. What we are doing is raising our energy in order to believe that when we walk on the coals, we will not be burned.

That night, gazing into the eyes of my friend Carin who stands across the circle, I stroll across the red embers. I do not get burned. It's an exhilarating feeling. A few people get third degree blister burns on the soles of their feet.

I've lived in fear all my life. *Look what I've done*. I can overcome fear.

I'm back at the nursing home; they've just brought my mom her dinner. My sister is feeding her.

Life is full of joys and challenges. I can focus on the challenges or I can focus on the joys. What I learned from the firewalk is no matter where I put my focus, the one ingredient most important before my mind's eye is gratitude. How very grateful I am to have these experiences. How special it is to see the smile on my mom's face as she talks about her grandchildren or her favorite bowl of clam chowder. Renewing my relationship with my sisters gives me joy. I'm growing with them again, sharing, laughing, dancing life together. We bring to our renewed relationships more wisdom than before and respect for ourselves. And of course, we share grandchildren stories.

But this still doesn't answer the tears within. I inhale slowly, closing my eyes. Thinking about my meditation CD, I breathe out.

HOW IT HELPS

Love is the most powerful force on this Earth. I wrote a mantra to help me feel safe and strong. These words help me hold this truth and have helped me know there's no need for fear. Fear is only as strong as my energy feeds it. Fear can be used to empower or to weaken. An acronym for fear is 'false evidence appearing real'. Fear can be used to control people. Controlling people leads to a misuse of power. Strength lies in love and truth, not in fear.

This is my mantra:

I AM A WOMAN FREE AND PROUD
OPENNESS IS MY BATTLEFIELD
TRUTH IS MY SWORD
FEAR IS MY ENEMY AND
GOD IS MY ALLY

Love is stronger than anything! We pray for the highest and best good to come out of any situation. When you feel like you're failing at everything, you're not. On some level, somewhere you're moving forward. Sometimes feeling out of control helps us find control. And as for gratitude—it's the window that gets us going.

EPILOGUE

Wednesday, April 2, 2014

Lisa is in liver failure and has been put on the liver transplant list at Massachusetts General Hospital (MGH). I don't know what to feel. It's finally happening.

She's been losing weight and became subjected to a type of brain fog that's caused by too much ammonia in one's blood. She's 32 years old. They tell me that the brain fog is only temporary but it's painful to watch. She also became seriously addicted to a painkiller called Dilaudid. She told me she tried to buy it on the street because her primary care doctor refused to refill her prescription.

She's been in and out of the hospital since January with liver pain and worrisome test results. She had to reduce her work hours to part-time because of her iffy medical state. Last month, they began doing the transplant evaluation. It included a psychiatric test to make sure she is not suicidal.

I take a breath and don't know how to let it out, thinking the dream of a normal life will dissipate if I do. More than likely, Massachusetts will not be able to supply the organ in a timely fashion so we need to look at out-of-state transplant centers to see who will help us.

End-stage liver disease is measured using a MELD score. A patient's state is assessed by adding up their serum bilirubin, serum creatinine, and the international normalized ratio for prothrombin time. It's a metric used to predict survival. High is not good. A score over

30 indicates a patient has a 50 percent chance of surviving three months. Lisa's MELD score is 16.

Thursday, April 10, 2014

Lisa has decided to go to Florida with her sister to visit their father. Over my objections, her gastroenterologist, Dr. Parker, okays the trip.

She stays at my house so that I can take her to Logan Airport. She lives about two hours from Boston; I live closer, near my work as an office manager. Overmedicated with narcotics, she's awake most of the night like a pacing dog. Her pain is severe and hard to control. I fall asleep and wake up at 3:00 a.m. She's trying hard to keep quiet. We try many things to help her relax but it isn't until I hold her in my arms that she finally falls asleep. We spoon each other in bed and she holds my arms around her. Usually, she doesn't want to be touched but she falls sound asleep, twitching and moaning through the early morning hours.

She stays in bed all day and gets herself together for her flight.

Friday, April 11, 2014

The reality of her getting a transplant is hitting me. There's so much we don't know. How will all this be paid for? She has insurance but has to stop working for now.

Elizabeth at the American Liver Foundation says to use the Foundation as a resource. I'm grateful. But I'm appalled to learn that we have to contact transplant centers ourselves. I thought some method was in place so we don't have to state our case individually to each center. Elizabeth gives us the contact information for three centers and also suggests we contact the National Foundation for Transplants as a fundraising resource.

We fill out the Social Security Disability Income (SSDI) form because even Lisa agrees she can't work anymore. It won't be long before she can't even live alone.

Wednesday, April 16, 2014

Lisa and Michelle return from Florida. We drive Lisa back to her own home. She says her most favorite time with her dad was when they sat under the lemon tree with a cold drink in their hands, listening to the birds.

Tuesday, April 22, 2014

Lisa wakes up with pain in her liver. Blood work is done and an infection is found. Family members rush Lisa the two hours to MGH and she's given two pints of blood. She has a drainage bag tapping into her liver. Her skin is becoming more and more yellow.

It's clear she has to get onto a shorter transplant list because she's losing ground. We're all contacting transplant centers, collecting whatever information we can.

The transplant hospitals in the United States are aggregated into 11 zones by the United Network for Organ Sharing. We learn that a patient can be on only one list in a zone. How are we going to be in Massachusetts and another state at the same time? And each hospital has its own characteristics: length of the list, how fast they get through the list, what MELD scores they'll accept. We scour the country for the shortest and fastest liver transplant list for her blood type and MELD score. It isn't Mass General.

Her pain level shoots up to a 10. The doctors remove five and a half liters of fluid from her abdomen as they deal with four different infections. They think her spleen has stopped working.

Thursday, May 8, 2014

Lisa is granted exception points to her MELD score so that it stands at 29. This is good for moving her up on the MGH transplant list.

Friday, May 9, 2014

Lisa's primary care doctor holds a special day for her. The whole staff dresses for the beach and they raise money for Lisa's transplant.

We've also set up a website page on the National Foundation for Transplants and have created our own website. An out-of-state transplant will be very expensive. Even if the insurance covers it, there'll be so many other expenses.

Sunday, May 11, 2014

Dr. Parker's office calls to inform us that Lisa is now second on the MGH list. I'm remembering that moment when she was 11 years old and we were at Tufts being evaluated for their transplant list. We're now second on a transplant list. Is this a moment where I can get my hopes up?

Wednesday, May 14, 2014

Lisa's pain meds and antibiotics have to be monitored but Dr. Parker says she's well enough to leave MGH while she waits for the transplant.

He has a gentle smile and a shock of black hair. His posture is a bit bent over from staring at microscopes too much. He continues. "But she's not well enough to be on her own or to even be at a general rehab facility."

"What should we do? Should she move in with me?"

Dr. Parker suggests an acute care facility and has Lisa moved to Spaulding Hospital.

Sunday, May 18, 2014

We just received word there's a liver available and Lisa is the backup for a possible transplant! The surgeon is going to Maine to harvest the organs. All day long, we try to act normal even though our reality is in someone else's hands far away. We wait and wait. I'm glad I'm not at work today, glad I'm retired from court reporting. I can barely concentrate. I try to breathe normally but cannot.

We wait without word. At 10:00 p.m., we find out that the liver has gone to someone else. It all feels hopeless. The roller coaster starts as I experience the cycles of chronic sorrow. I take a deep breath.

Thursday, May 22, 2014

Spaulding is a great facility for Lisa. Every day, she's getting occupational and physical therapy. The staff is giving her a low-sodium diet and restricting her water intake. She gets blood transfusions when she needs them and all her meds are given to her at the right intervals. She's wearing compression socks and trying to find ways to keep her mouth from drying out. Lisa has the type of outgoing personality that makes friends easily, even with her stutter. The staff is delighted with her attitude and sense of humor. She's got nurses and other staff laughing and joking around with her.

Sunday, June 1, 2014

Lisa's pain is increasing in spite of all the pain meds. Her actual MELD score now stands at 20.

Monday, June 2, 2014

At 1:00 a.m., Lisa calls in agony, saying she's in pain and the night doctor wants to give her Motrin. I rush to Spaulding and ask to see the doctor. When he comes to Lisa's floor, I am calm but insistent—she needs to go back to MGH. He says the pain med will be enough. I want to remind him that he's thought about her situation for one minute while I could list all the pain meds she's been on for years. *I'm a walking database and know Motrin can be toxic to people in advanced liver disease.*

I stare him down until he relents. An ambulance takes Lisa back to MGH. She's crying all the way there.

The ICU doctors determine her colon is impacted in spite of having some bowel movements, and she is admitted for treatment.

Tuesday, June 3, 2014

Dr. Parker says that at this point in her illness, the only intervention that will give meaningful benefit is a liver transplant; everything else is temporizing. He suggests Indiana University Hospital in Indianapolis; they have a very high rate of getting through their transplant list because they're the only recipient from an organ procurement center in Zone 10.

Friday, June 6, 2014

We hold a big fundraiser for Lisa's transplant. Lisa is too ill to attend, but she cries tears of joy when she hears how much money is raised through her community of friends and family.

Tuesday, June 10, 2014

We have contacted Indiana University Hospital and gotten all Lisa's records faxed to them. They currently have 56 people on their liver transplant list, although the number with Lisa's blood type is much smaller. There are so many unknowns—but it's almost a dream. For so many years, she was getting by without a transplant; even though she was sick every year, she was never sick enough to need a transplant. And now, here we are, about to get onto a second transplant list.

How are we going to get to Indianapolis?

Thursday, June 12, 2014

Lisa is discharged from MGH and we take her to her sister's house. She cannot live alone in her own apartment in her brain-fogged state. She needs to stay home-bound, and she needs a visiting nurse, occupational therapy, physical therapy, and her drainage bags monitored. Michelle and Eric rearrange their house to accommodate her and we order a hospital bed.

I'm so distracted. I'm making mistakes at work. I don't know how I can continue working knowing how much care she needs. Her drainage tubes are a constant challenge with bile leaking onto her clothes. I want to be with her.

Friday, June 13, 2014

I go into my boss's office and quit my job. He understands and says it's for the best. I can now devote myself to Lisa's full-time care. This is the only way I will stay sane. I've got food in the fridge and the rent is paid. I'm going to stay present, grounded, and centered. How this will all work is a big blinking "I don't know" sign.

Michelle has made an emergency protocol document and distributed it to all the people involved in Lisa's care-giving shifts. Other family members are making low-sodium food for Lisa in order to make mealtime easy on everyone. Michelle has a full-time job plus two small children to care for. I go to Michelle's every day to take care of Lisa's necessities. If I am not there, friends and other family members stop in.

Wednesday, June 25, 2014

The summer is becoming a scorcher with temperatures in the nineties. Lisa takes short walks up and down the street with her niece and nephew. Dr. Parker says her labs are looking good, her sodium is stable and pain under control. Her drainage bag continues to leak but new meds are helping her alertness.

The transplant coordinator from Indiana University Hospital calls and tells us Lisa's four-day evaluation will take place at the end of July. They had to schedule appointments with hepatology, cardiology, the surgeon, and a psych evaluation. They are still not certain about the scheduling for all the tests. They'll let us know. Also, before she goes, she has to get a mammogram, a pap smear, an endoscopy, and a dental checkup. When they give someone another person's organs, they want to make sure that that the recipient is otherwise healthy.

It all seems impossible, but everyone is helping to make this work. Money is coming in to help out. We make airline and car reservations. I'll be taking her to Indiana.

In one of my daily visits to Michelle's house, I check Lisa's medication supply. She has Dilaudid (a street narcotic) on hand. I notice about 30 pills missing.

After questioning Lisa, who assures us she did not take them, we query everyone involved. We have to call the police and an investigation ensues. After a lengthy bit of questioning, we have no conclusion: maybe one of the home care providers, maybe one of the friends. We have no proof who took them and no resolution.

My heart breaks thinking how Lisa is being compromised by someone else's addiction. Now, we have to make more frequent visits to the drugstore because the prescription amounts have to be smaller.

Saturday, June 28, 2014

I walk in the American Liver Foundation's Liver Life Walk in Boston. I'm doing it to raise awareness of pediatric liver disease.

Tuesday, July 8, 2014

The visiting nurse arrives and checks Lisa's vitals. Lisa's oxygen saturation is too low. An ambulance is called and rushes Lisa to MGH. Her blood pressure is dropping. I sit in the front seat of the ambulance hating the sound of the siren.

The doctors stabilize her in the ICU. Her pain level shoots up to a 10.

Monday, July 14, 2014

Lisa is quite colorful with bags of green, red, and yellow fluids draining from her. She shows us her high-tech bed that lets her sit up like in a chair.

Saturday, July 19, 2014

Lisa is transferred to the main hospital floor. She has a self-administering pump for her pain medications and a chest tube to drain fluids from her chest.

I discover that MGH has a healing garden on the top of one of the buildings. I take Lisa up there in a wheelchair. There are trees and flowers and a rock garden. I love the peacefulness of it. Afterwards, I take her to the specialty gift shop to find scarves she can wear because her hair is falling out from all the medications she's taking.

Friday, July 25, 2014

We're getting more and more worried about Lisa's state. She's been cleared to travel, but her hematocrit is low and she's on IV antibiotics. We may have to postpone her trip to Indiana. How can she travel on an airplane in this state?

We receive a call from the head of the Indiana University (IU) transplant surgery. Dr. Tacker wants to interview Lisa on August 6th, do a two-day evaluation, and list her immediately. I cry with relief. Now we just have to figure out how to get her there.

Tuesday, July 29, 2014

A friend suggests we look into air ambulances. After some misinformation, I find out that it's possible and apply for an authorization from the insurance company.

Wednesday, July 30, 2014

While walking out of the bathroom in her hospital room, Lisa trips and breaks the humerus bone in her arm. Luckily, it's a clean compression break and won't require surgery. They immobilize her arm in a dark blue splint. She has bruises on her back and left arm from the fall. She's now in additional pain from the break.

Thursday, July 31, 2014

We got insurance approval for the air ambulance! We cancel the commercial airline flights. With her broken arm, this seems like the only workable way.

Friday, August 1, 2014

I'm at MGH with Lisa. The doctors decide that she has to go to Indiana immediately, that there is no reason to wait and every reason to get her on her way. They pack up her meds and give her a larger arm splint. Friends throw together a small suitcase for me and drive it into Boston to MGH.

A half hour later, Lisa and I are in an ambulance heading out to Hanscom Air Force Base where we board a Learjet which flies us to Indianapolis. I watch the lights of Boston retreat in the distance, remembering that first frantic drive into the city in 1981. *We're one step closer.*

Arriving in Indianapolis, an ambulance takes us to the IU hospital. By 11:00 p.m., Lisa is admitted, and I take a taxi to a long-term residence hotel about three miles away. Families of the hospital patients stay there.

I take a deep breath. Everything is working. We got her to a center where a transplant can happen quickly enough for her, even with a broken arm.

I feel an inkling of hope. We made it happen. I'm exhausted but keep putting one foot in front of the other. I've assembled so many tools over the years. *I'm needing every one of them.*

Sunday, August 3, 2014

Mark arrived this afternoon. It's been a whirlwind of meeting doctors, having X-rays, changing dressings, getting her history, connecting this team with the MGH doctors. Right now, they're just trying to stabilize her in preparation for the evaluation.

We take Lisa in a wheelchair for a roll around the transplant unit. Today is her 100th day being hospitalized this year.

I'm still stunned that we've come this far. She's finally going to get a transplant.

Wednesday, August 6, 2014

They've begun the evaluation. She's had many tests done: X-rays, CT scans, Doppler ultrasound, pulmonary function test, a mammogram. All are incredibly painful because of her broken arm. Her drainage bag leaks bile continuously. She has a dental exam and also a cardio evaluation. She's given three vaccines. The scariest problem is that they can't clearly see her portal vein, which is something they need for the transplant. They think this vital vein is clotted off.

While in the ICU kitchen, Dr. Tacker grabs small packets of peanut butter for his dinner and he asks me to walk with him. "We may need to do a multi-visceral transplant."

"What's that mean?" I'm matching my steps to his.

"Not just her liver, but her pancreas, stomach, small and large intestines."

These words bring up echoes from so long ago. Her first diagnosis, her foreign object. I take a breath, try to find another one. My heart starts to pound.

He insists they're quite familiar with this operation, doing about 40 of these a year. Once she gets listed, she'll be prioritized. "She'll get the transplant within 30 to 45 days. We'll start the search for the organs."

"The search?"

"Yeah, nationally. Meanwhile, she's stable enough to be discharged from the hospital."

Thursday, August 7, 2014

Mark and I settle Lisa into my room at the residence hotel. Lisa calls Michelle about 10:30 p.m. and we all talk as a family. This is hard on all of us, especially Michelle being so far away.

After the call, Lisa doesn't want to go to sleep. Mark doesn't want to go to sleep either. I can't go to sleep until she does, so it isn't until 3:00 a.m. that we all fall asleep.

Friday, August 8, 2014

It's always hard on Lisa when Mark leaves. He heads out before 7:00 a.m. for his flight.

I start the routine of pills, drainage, meals, and primary care. With her broken arm, she's very compromised. But other members of our extended family come for a visit and help us get organized. I go shopping for groceries. The home healthcare company comes by and delivers medical conveniences—a commode, a shower bench, and supplies for her drainage bags. Lisa sits with a clothespin on her nose to stop yet another bloody nose.

Tuesday, August 12, 2014

Her insurance has approved her for a transplant! Step by step, each piece is falling into place. Now we are waiting to hear that she's formally on the multi-visceral transplant (MVT) list. We've had a visiting nurse come twice since we left the hospital. I've managed to give Lisa a shower. She's had a couple more nosebleeds. The physical therapist gave her exercises to do three times a day because she's in danger of falling.

Thursday, August 14, 2014

Today is our first time at the IU transplant clinic to meet our transplant coordinator and learn what other tests Lisa needs. She's on the transplant list! Somehow we did it. Lisa will be going to these clinics weekly up until her transplant and then continuing on afterwards.

The surgery may take up to 10 hours. Their first goal will be to free the portal vein of the clot to see if it is usable. They hope to just transplant her liver, but will have to plan for a multi-visceral transplant in case. She will be in the ICU from three to 10 days and then on the transplant floor for a month. The risk of rejection is five times with a MVT as each organ system can have its own rejection.

She's the only person with her blood type on the waiting list for an MVT, so she's number one. She must be compliant with fluid and food restrictions. There's no room for any screwing around.

Sunday, August 17, 2014

We've been enjoying our days together, even though they're emotionally exhausting. It takes a couple of hours to shower her because of the drainage bags, IV ports, and broken arm.

We've also been receiving care packages from friends and family members. The packages make things a bit easier. One had a jigsaw puzzle with bright frogs on it. We've started putting it together. Two days ago, we received an anonymous card from God. There was no postmark to help us figure out where it was sent from. It said this:

"You have done a beautiful job of teaching compassion and patience and love. Your spiritual journey may have seemed difficult at times but I knew you were the only one who could do it with such style. I will not let you leave the planet and return to me until you have completed all the requirements of your life purpose. You have more to learn and more to teach. Carry on, brave daughter. Love, God."

Lisa likes the card and cries because it makes me cry. It certainly is moving. We post it on our website.

But by the afternoon, I realize something is not quite right with Lisa. I talk to the transplant coordinator and they send an ambulance. Lisa is rushed back to the hospital with low blood pressure and a rising temperature. She barely knows her own name. She's admitted into the hospital and a central line is put in to administer BP meds. She starts on more antibiotics.

Tuesday, August 19, 2014

Lisa gets approval from her insurance company for a multi-visceral transplant. The final piece has fallen into place. I feel a rush of emotions. The waiting game starts in earnest.

Wednesday, August 20, 2014

Lisa has been in a brain fog from all the ammonia in her body. The nurses say it's been hard to wake her up in the morning. She has a blood infection and fluid is building up in her lungs. A chest X-ray shows she has aspiration pneumonia. If her breathing doesn't improve, they're going to intubate her, which means sticking a tube into her windpipe to help her breathe. Her blood pressure has been dropping.

Thursday, August 21, 2014

Michelle is arriving today for a visit. On the way to the airport, I receive a phone call from the transplant coordinator—they have an offer of a donor available. That means someone with Lisa's blood type has died and the organs have been offered for Lisa. The transplant surgeon is dispatched to the body to assess the condition. If the organs are viable, she will be on the operating table tonight. I call Mark and tell him the news.

Lisa is so excited to see her sister. We all hug and hug so much. But it's so hard. Lisa cannot eat anymore so they're feeding her by a tube.

In the evening, we find out the donor's organs were not viable and so they're not available. It's disheartening to be so close, seeing the end in sight, but not being able to cross the finish line. We are all devastated. Fifteen days ago, Dr. Tacker had said it would take 30 to 45 days. Was this our last chance?

Friday, August 22, 2014

Lisa's kidneys are in trouble. I sit in the clinical manager's office crying over this news. She says that they aren't failing, but Lisa's creatinine levels are rising, possibly because of all the meds. With her lungs not doing well either, I ask Dr. Tacker how Lisa is going to survive. He says you have to hang in there, it's a squeeze but the patients get through it. This transplant unit handles some of the most difficult cases in the world. Mark arrives in the evening.

Saturday, August 23, 2014

In the morning, Lisa is stable. She has a coloring book that came in one of the care packages and she's coloring in it. Michelle, Mark, and I spend the day with her.

In the evening, Lisa starts a low-grade temperature of 99.8. She has more and more trouble breathing, and finally at 10:00 p.m., the doctors intubate her. It's so hard to see this big tube in her mouth. She speaks with her eyes now. The tube gives her lungs a chance to relax and recover. The ICU nurses are extremely attentive to her, keeping her as comfortable as they can.

Sunday, August 24, 2014

Michelle leaves in the morning. It's hard for her to pull away but she has a job, a husband, and two small children.

Since Lisa can no longer talk because of the tube, Mark and his wife Glenda get her some paper and markers. Lisa is awake enough to write notes. The first thing she writes is, "I want nails done." Glenda does her nails with a metallic polish called 'Heroic'.

The doctors do an ultrasound of her lungs and inject a saline solution to clean them out. Her kidneys remain stable at the moment. Her MELD score is 38 and she's glowing yellow. She is heroically getting through this, as are all the members of the family and friends who are helping and making this bearable.

Wednesday, August 27, 2014

I find out today that Lisa's not on the transplant waiting list while she's intubated. I'm devastated by this news. We've worked so hard to ready her for the transplant, flown hundreds of miles, sacrificed our time and effort for this, spent a lot of our money and our friends' money. We begin to watch every measurement the doctors take, looking for positive trends towards removing the tube.

They try letting her breathe on her own even with the tube. We stare at the graphs and monitor the numbers. They're trending in the right direction. The respiratory therapist suctions her, bringing out phlegm from her lungs. But after an hour, they switch her back to full ventilator support. It's good exercise for her lungs and will repeat it as the days progress.

In the afternoon, they take her to the hospital's basement to the barium kitchen to reposition the feeding tube. It's quite an ordeal. All the wires, cables and tubes coming from Lisa are gathered up, and a nurse and two techs push her bed, her ventilator, her IV bags, her meds, and a few extra machines down the hallways to the elevators. It's like a parade with me and Mark following them.

Saturday, August 30, 2014

Lisa has a new draining tube put in to drain the bile. The doctors are trying to figure out if she has an infection in her lungs. She's breathing too fast and not getting normal volumes of oxygen. They have started her on antibiotics in addition to the blood pressure, pain killers, and all the other medications.

Lisa had a hard time sleeping last night. She knows her dad is leaving today. Her creatinine level is high and she's not putting out much urine; they will likely put her on dialysis tomorrow. This will increase her MELD score which is good in terms of getting closer to a transplant. But as long as she has an infection and is on the ventilator, she's on the Inactive list.

Sunday, August 31, 2014

Lisa was agitated during the night and had to be restrained. At 8:00 in the morning, I find out Lisa's lungs are now in a state of Adult Respiratory Distress Syndrome. She's not getting enough oxygen when breathing on her own. At the same time, her creatinine is much higher than expected.

They transfer her to a Triadyne bed which will help her breathe. It rotates her 40 degrees left and right in order to move the fluids in her lungs around.

An hour later, the dialysis team arrives and puts her on dialysis through her femoral artery. It's to give her kidneys a rest, they say. Her face looks puffy and red. They're going to give her a sedative.

The dialysis machine makes a sound like bells. I had heard the sound from other places on the unit's floor but didn't know what it was. Now I do.

In the afternoon, we're informed that her chest X-ray is worse. It will take time for the dialysis to pull all this junk from her lungs.

Monday, September 1, 2014

The doctors come by on their rounds. They explain that, before dialysis, her fluid output was not sufficient for the amount of fluid going in. Now the dialysis is drawing fluid off from her lungs. They say that her lungs are severely damaged. They don't want patients on a ventilator more than two weeks. If her lungs don't improve, they'll do a tracheotomy. But the transplant doctor says he expects her lungs to get better because she's making good progress.

At 10:00 a.m., the nurses put her into a medically-induced coma in order to give her a bath. Lisa throws up blood and they suction up all this dark stuff. They give her a unit of blood.

For a few minutes, her heart rate goes up to 170 and her blood pressure drops. But both stabilize.

Tuesday, September 2, 2014

Lisa is still in the medically-induced coma in order to reduce the stress on her body. But her heart rate jumps up a few times into atrial fibrillation. The nurses shock her heart into rhythm.

I'm trying to not freak out. They think Lisa is dried out. They start her on more albumen. Things don't improve and the transplant surgeons arrive along with doctors from Pharmacy and Cardiology. More nurses arrive. They shock her twice more. They're all consulting in a huddle, trying to figure out what to do. Her oxygen is increased, ultrasounds and an echocardiogram done. Everything they try does not get her heart back to normal.

But by 6:00 p.m., the episodes finally stop. We're all hollow-eyed in shock and stare at her peaceful sleeping form.

Wednesday, September 3, 2014

In the morning, Lisa has an episode of vomiting. A blood culture indicates that she is septic.

Mark arrives around noon. We have a family meeting with the transplant doctor who says Lisa is limping along in the right direction. He thinks her kidneys will recover. She has to be less dependent on the ventilator and achieve some improvement in her lungs.

Lisa has a set of angel cards, each one with a message. The one we pick today is 'divine intervention'.

Thursday, September 4, 2014

While Lisa is in the induced coma, Mark plays a video of Lisa's niece and nephew laughing and playing. Lisa's brain function jumps up several points as Mark holds the iPhone up to her ear. It's wonderful to see the response. We're expecting her to come back to consciousness kicking and screaming, wanting ice chips and demanding to walk. The nurses are ready. Once her breathing tube is removed, she will have to be evaluated for swallowing and ice chips will be the first thing into her mouth. She will be thrilled, but fluid control is of utmost importance. Transplant surgeons are waiting for the window of opportunity to have the transplant. Now we need the organs.

Michelle and her husband leave in the morning. Lisa's blood sugar is skyrocketing but her lungs are looking good. The doctors say that the heart roller coaster she has been on is probably due to the blood pressure meds. They start lowering the Nimbex that has kept her in a coma. At noon, she starts stirring and they put her back into a regular hospital bed.

Friday, September 5, 2014

Even though Lisa is on the ventilator, she's breathing on her own. At 9:00 a.m., the transplant doctor says he's pleased and that she's out of the woods.

At about 1:00 p.m., she opens her eyes. She's dazed and moves her arms and blankly stares at everyone. Mark plays the video of Jackson for her again. By the afternoon, she's coherent and upset about the ventilator. Her eyes scream with her anger, wanting the tube removed. They put restraints on her so that she doesn't pull out the cables and tubes.

Saturday, September 6, 2014

They take the ventilator tube out. Lisa tries to speak but doesn't make much sense. She's pretty exhausted. And cold. The dialysis causes chills and she needs extra blankets.

It's hard to tell whether she's aware of what's going on as she's so tired. She continues to be cold even with heated blankets piled on her. I want to bring in the handmade quilt, a gift from my sister. Lisa seems aware I'm here but then, at times, I wonder. I talk with her as if she's listening.

Sunday, September 7, 2014

I go to the All Souls Unitarian Church. It's about 20 minutes away from the hotel. The sanctuary is large and filled with light. The people are friendly and the music great and comforting.

I find out tonight Lisa has a urinary tract infection and is on antibiotics. It's my plan to be at rounds tomorrow morning and ask the doctors when she'll be back on the active transplant list.

She deserves a break at this point.

Monday, September 8, 2014

The transplant surgeons tell me that Lisa's kidneys are shot. To save her lungs, she was put on dialysis which affected her kidneys. There was no choice. If she were to have an MVT without replacing a kidney, she would not survive. She's completely dependent on dialysis now 24/7. This means she will have the MVT one day and a kidney transplant the next day.

So we move onward. We ask everyone we know to keep praying for a donor, because we're running out of time.

Tuesday, September 9, 2014

Lisa has been antsy, wanting to get out of the bed. She hasn't been able to be mobile because of the dialysis. Doctors have heard her and are doing two procedures tomorrow. The access for dialysis will be moved from her femoral to her clavicle area, and her central line will be moved to a more permanent space in her chest. Both of these procedures will allow her mobility. PT will start working with her shortly thereafter to get her up and walking. Her fighting spirit is what helped them make this decision.

Wednesday, September 10, 2014

Her kidneys are making urine! She was off dialysis today to give her a break. If she continues, they'll put her on dialysis three times a week instead of 24/7. We're making progress!

And, the insurance company approved the addition of the kidney transplant. She'll be officially listed as of tonight. The doctor also okayed her to have ice chips as long as she doesn't cough and aspirate.

I finally remember to ask the liaison nurses if there's Reiki in the hospital. Nobody on the staff knows about this touch therapy. But in my questioning, I find out there is music therapy.

Physical therapists help Lisa sit up. She's a rag doll with no energy, but the PT seems to bring her to life. It's a beginning. At the end of the day, Lisa is beyond exhausted but we feel that things are moving in a positive direction.

Thursday, September 11, 2014

The music therapist Dan comes by this morning. He is delightful, pulling a roll cart with a guitar. It holds an iPad and he can look up any music. He takes a seat and starts playing songs I like and takes requests of Lisa's favorites. He keeps Lisa's attention, and though she doesn't talk much, she's listening. When he sings her favorite, *At Last*, by Etta James, I see her moving her lips. That makes it all worth it. I find myself harmonizing with Dan.

Unfortunately, after about 40 minutes, Lisa has a nosebleed which ends the music session.

Friday, September 12, 2014

The renal doctors are delighted that Lisa is making urine, but she's not pulling out the toxins that cause problems, so therefore she's scheduled for dialysis today. The transplant team is doing everything they can to keep her kidneys engaged.

Two friends from the All Souls Church come to visit. I have hot chocolate with them. The temperature has changed here in Indianapolis. It feels like autumn at 55 degrees. The physical therapist comes by and gets Lisa to sit on the side of the bed for 10 minutes. Then the dialysis team comes and engages her for the next four hours.

Saturday, September 13, 2014

Lisa seems stabilized. Her IV pole is not hanging as many drugs as it was previously. She's not had a positive culture in 10 days. That's the good news. It's all relatively speaking as she's unable to eat, talk, or walk, and is being fed through a feeding tube and has an ammonia level so high she's disoriented and confused. But she's not on oxygen and gets breathing exercises from the respiratory therapists three times a day. That's a vast improvement. PT is helping her move to the side of the bed with a goal of eventually standing up. She sits in a cardiac chair for 45 minutes.

We are waiting for organs.

Sunday, September 14, 2014

I go to the Unitarian Church again. I'm getting to know people there and they are all helpful, friendly and welcoming. I've been in Indianapolis a while now and have made some great connections.

I'm back at the hospital by 1:00 p.m. The nurse and I have figured out Lisa's silent communications. When she throws her covers off and hangs her legs off the side of the bed, she's generally uncomfortable. It's her way of saying she's in pain. Today we got her her pain medication sooner.

Lisa needs dialysis, not the four-hour kind, but all day. The nurse brings in an EKG machine and says Lisa is in afib again. Her heart rate is bouncing from 118 to 160.

The doctors decide to do an IV heart rate med and to increase her potassium. It takes about 15 minutes to get her heart rate under control. We'll hear tomorrow from the cardio doctors if there's any damage to her heart.

She's stable again. We wait.

Tuesday, September 16, 2014

At about 4:00 p.m., we hear there's a possibility of organs for Lisa. We won't know anything more until very, very late tonight.

I'm back at the hotel and can barely sleep. It's been 41 days since Dr. Tacker said she will get the transplant within 30 to 45 days. This is it.

Wednesday, September 17, 2014

At 3:00 a.m., I receive the call. The possible organs won't work for Lisa. The stomach was not suitable for transplant, and to ensure success, they have to have all the organs. I'm crying but there are no words for this. One can live in a place called 'if only' but where will that get me. We can still receive another call. The transplant can still happen.

At 10:00 a.m., Lisa's blood pressure drops to 86/41. She's put on IV blood pressure meds. They think it's because she got too dry again. It's a fine balancing act, keeping her close to dehydration but not totally dehydrated. By the end of the day, Lisa's blood pressure is responding to the meds.

One of the nurses tells me to not lose hope. She's worked at the hospital for five years and she said hope and faith are the strong threads that help them all hang in there. I believe in the doctors and the nurses. They've proved beyond a shadow of a doubt that they know what they're doing.

Dr. Friedman comes by and tells me he's anxious to get organs for Lisa. He feels that she's in good shape with her lungs, and even though her bilirubin is so high, the transplant is still possible; they just have to work harder.

In the afternoon, the music therapist Dan comes by again. Together, we sing to Lisa. Whether Lisa can hear it or not, at least it gives me some comfort.

Thursday, September 18, 2014

About 2:00 p.m., Lisa's blood pressure starts dropping and so does her blood sugar. She becomes unconscious. The doctors determine she is in sepsis with a blood infection. They begin removing any equipment that could be the source of the infection.

They give her blood plasma but it hasn't helped. She starts vomiting blood and also pooping blood. She falls into a coma.

When she is stabilized, the doctors all leave. Only a nurse and I remain. I am standing by Lisa's bedside.

I ask the nurse to check her because she seems too quiet. The nurse agrees with me. She confirms her heart is beating. We wait for any sign of improvement.

At about 10:30 p.m., they take her downstairs for a brain CT scan to determine her brain function.

I'm in the waiting room talking on my cell phone. Over the loudspeaker, I hear a voice, "Code blue in CT scan."

I scream and drop the phone. I know it's her. I begin sobbing uncontrollably. A nurse appears at the door and escorts me down to the scan room. The room is full of medical people attempting to resuscitate Lisa.

A nurse asks me if I want to go in and see her.

"No." It's done. She's gone. I can feel it.

They pronounce Lisa dead at 11:00 p.m. She is 32 years old.

Saturday, September 20, 2014

Family members have arrived. We hold a small memorial in the hospital chapel. Dan, the music therapist, plays Lisa's favorite songs. Nurses from the transplant floor attend. The minister from All Souls Unitarian Church is here as well.

We're all exhausted and heartbroken. Lisa put up one hell of a fight. My only comfort is to know she is out of pain. She is free of her broken body.

Whether a child is born into this life with a disease like Lisa was, or acquires a disease after birth, we as parents are left with the task of caring for them. We can choose to abandon ourselves and devote our entire life to caring for the ill child. Or we can take care of ourselves while caring for the child and dealing with the illness.

I made a conscious choice to be a whole person. My childhood was not a picnic and I had to heal from many deep wounds. But I committed myself to caring for my children in the way I would have wanted to be cared for, to feel the nurturing parental love and respect I yearned for.

For Lisa, I educated myself in all aspects of her illness, became her advocate, bonded with her, and cared for her. For Michelle, our bond grew stronger and stronger as she grew from child to adult to becoming a parent herself. As for myself, I chose to learn a functional and thriving way of life despite the ongoing pressures of chronic illness and chronic sorrow.

I miss Lisa. There are still days when I can only cry. But in looking back, I have no regrets. There was nothing left unsaid, there was nothing left undone. I know I did everything a parent could have done. And I am at peace today celebrating my life and the lives of my beautiful daughters and grandchildren.

PUBLISHED RESOURCES

BOOKS

Eden, Donna. *Energy Medicine*, NY: Jeremy P. Turcher/Putnam, 1998.

Jeffers, Susan. *Feel the Fear and Do It Anyway*, NY: Ballantine Books, 1987 (and 2007).

Tolle, Eckhart. *A New Earth*. NY: Penguin Group, 2005.

WEBSITES

www.braingym.org – brain calming exercises using educational kinesiology

www.chronicsorrow.org – chronic sorrow

www.louisehay.com - Louise Hay's books and CDs

www.siblingsupport.org/sibshops - sibling workshops

www.our-kids.org/archives/Holland.html - *Welcome to Holland* essay by Emily Perl Kingsley

https://www.youtube.com/watch?v=e9lfi7gCuz0 – Fred Small's Everything Possible song

www.tomatis.com – Tomatis Method

www.lindaworster.com - Linda Worster, musician

www.psychologytoday.com – Psychology Today Magazine

www.emotionalfreedomtechniques.net - Emotional Freedom Technique (EFT)

www.firewalking.com - Firewalking

www.liverfoundation.org - American Liver Foundation

www.unos.org – United Network for Organ Sharing